# The High Cost
# of Farm Welfare

# The High Cost of Farm Welfare

## Clifton B. Luttrell

CATO
INSTITUTE
Washington, D.C.

**Library of Congress Cataloging-in-Publication Data**

Luttrell, Clifton B.
  The high cost of farm welfare / Clifton B. Luttrell.
     p.   cm.  ·
  Bibliography: p. 131
  Includes index.
    1. Agricultural subsidies—United States.   2. Agriculture and state—
United States.   3. Agriculture—Economic aspects—United States.   I. Title.
HD1761.L87   1989            338.1'8—dc19
ISBN 0-932790-70-4.                                                    88-34439
ISBN 0-932790-71-2 (pbk.)                                                CIP

Printed in the United States of America.

CATO INSTITUTE
224 Second Street SE
Washington, D.C. 20003

# Contents

PREFACE                                                                    ix

ACKNOWLEDGMENTS                                                            xiii

1. BIRTH OF THE FARM PROGRAMS                                               1

2. A NEW DEAL FOR AGRICULTURE EMERGES                                      13

3. THE FIRST PHASE: SUPPLY MANAGEMENT                                      21

4. WHY SUPPLY MANAGEMENT FAILED                                            31

5. THE SECOND PHASE: SURPLUS PROBLEMS AND EXPORT
   SUBSIDIES                                                               43

6. THE THIRD PHASE: DIRECT PAYMENTS                                        55

7. FOOD STAMPS AND FARMERS                                                 61

8. SUBSIDIZED CREDIT: WORSENING FARM POVERTY AND
   FARM DEBT PROBLEMS                                                      69

9. THE DAIRY PROGRAM: MILKING THE TAXPAYERS                                89

10. THE SUGAR PROGRAM: SWEET DEAL FOR PRODUCERS                            99

11. THE HIGH-COST WAY TO AID LOW-INCOME FARMERS                           113

REFERENCES                                                                131

APPENDIX                                                                  135

INDEX                                                                     145

# Tables

3.1 Acreage, Yield, and Production of Selected Crops before and after AAA   22

3.2 Annual Rates of Change in Acres, Yield, and Production of Selected Crops   24

3.3 CCC Holdings of Major Commodities, Owned plus Amount Pledged for Price Support Loans   26

4.1 Production and Exports of Upland Cotton   34

4.2 Government Support Prices of Selected Farm Commodities   35

4.3 U.S. and World Exports of Cotton   36

4.4 Rates of Change, Average Price Received for Farm Products Sold and Average Price Paid for Items Used in Farm Production   37

4.5 Trend in Use of Primary Plant Nutrients   39

4.6 Average Cost of USDA Programs and Wholesale Price Index   40

5.1 CCC Loan Rates on Major Commodities   46

5.2 Commercial and Government-Assisted Agricultural Exports before and after P.L.480   49

7.1 Cost of and Participation in Food Stamp and Commodity Distribution Programs   64

8.1 Farm Real Estate Debt by Reporting Lender   72

8.2 Non–Real Estate Debt   73

8.3 Active FmHA Loans   76

8.4 Change in Farmland Value and Farm Real Estate Debt Held by Selected Lenders   79

9.1 Dairy Products Removed from Commercial Markets by Government Purchases   90

9.2 Milk Diversion Payments: Top Five States, January 1984 to April 1985   95

10.1 U.S. Sugar Production, Use, and Imports       100

10.2 U.S. Sugar Crops: Acreage, Yield, and Production by
State, 1985       101

10.3 U.S. Consumption of Caloric Sweeteners       103

10.4 Average Price of Sugar Abroad and in the United
States       105

10.5 U.S. Production, Imports, and Consumption of
Caloric Sweeteners       107

10.6 Prices of Refined Sugar and High-Fructose Corn
Syrup (HFCS)       108

11.1 Farm Income by Size of Farm, 1985       114

11.2 Direct Government Payments to Farmers by
Sales Class       118

11.3 Federal Outlays for Farm Income Maintenance, 1985       119

11.4 Annual Gains and Losses from Farm Income-Support
Programs under 1985 Food Security Act       122

11.5 Potential Social Cost of Farm Programs in the Long
Run       124

11.6 All U.S. Families and Farm Families by Income and
Estimated Poverty Deficit, 1985       126

A-1 USDA Outlays as Percentage of Federal Government
Outlays and Net Farm Income       136

A-2 Realized Government Losses on Farm Price, Income
Support, and Related Programs       138

A-3 Direct Government Payments by Program       140

A-4 Support Price and Market Price for Farmers, Major
Crops       141

# Preface

In recent years, even taxpayers and consumers who think John Deere is an alias have had to take an interest in U.S. farm policy. Direct taxpayer costs of our current farm program amount to over $400 per family every year. In addition, there are the higher prices we pay at the cash register for our food and fiber. And there are the odd distortions. Like government grain rotting in temporary bunkers thrown up all around the Midwest. Like unexpected distributions of free cheese. Like farmers being paid to slaughter their dairy cows and go out of business. Like other farmers being paid to raise that venerable American weed, tobacco. Americans are beginning to realize that government interventions into agriculture are producing some weird, often disturbing, and extremely costly effects.

Government farm programs have existed for as long as farmers have been going out of business, which is most of this century. They really began to wind up with the advent of Franklin Roosevelt's New Deal in the 1930s. Their development since has been a steady upward spiral. World War II brought special "emergency" measures to support farm production. The Korean War did likewise. When our government sowing subsidies began to reap surpluses that were unmanageable, it nobly set up a massive "Food for Peace" program, which masked the dumping of excess American foodstuffs on underdeveloped nations (to the detriment of their own farmers) behind humanitarian rhetoric.

But Uncle Sam's blundering excursion into the world of gentleman farming really began to accelerate in the late 1960s and the 1970s. Having tinkered with a wide variety of crop loans, price supports, indirect subsidies, and whatnot, the Agriculture Department began to experiment with direct payments to farmers. Direct payments in return for promises to retire land. Direct payments to achieve a guaranteed crop price. Direct payments to do any number of specific things with one's milk cows.

This strategy reached its formal conclusion in the Payment-in-Kind (PIK) program of the early 1980s. Under this interesting plan, farmers were convinced not to grow foodstuffs by being paid off in foodstuffs the government had bought from them in earlier years. The effect was sort of like getting your slow-witted brother to buy a hound dog from you, then convincing him to give it back later because it was so obnoxious to keep, and besides he didn't want you to bring another one of those troublesome things home. This type of dealing proved enormously expensive for the government.

The one advantage of direct payments to farmers was that they allowed taxpayers to get some idea of just who exactly was reaping the benefits of the farm program. Many taxpayers were not amused to learn that most of the financial gains go to farmers with at least six-digit gross annual sales—not poor people. This was a critical insight, for the government farm programs were originally designed with the objective of improving the welfare and social standing of poor farmers. Farm people have long been thought to be structurally disadvantaged in comparison with other occupations. The goal of government subsidies was to allow farming families to achieve "parity" in their standard of living with nonfarming families in the industrial economy.

In fact, this study finds, farmers are not grossly poorer than nonfarmers. Nor do they operate under some separate code of returns. Farmers do what they do because they find it economically and otherwise rewarding. Government attempts to pump up average farm income will not have much lasting effect on average earnings; they will just draw more individuals into farming. The returns to farming in this country are largely predetermined by how much the relevant resource inputs (the farmer's labor, land, and capital, primarily) could earn elsewhere in the American economy. You are swimming against a very strong stream when you try to pay a redundant farmer to remain a farmer rather than become a car dealer.

If eliminating farm poverty were the only goal of U.S. agricultural policy, it could be done relatively cheaply—for about $4 billion at most—simply by sending payments directly to families below the poverty line. By doing it instead with price supports and so forth, we end up sending some fat checks to retirees living in the Virgin Islands who happen to own a 1,000-acre ranch.

But of course, our farm policy aims for more than just the elimination of rural poverty. It aims to preserve the family farm as a valuable social institution. It has bought urban support through a food stamp program, which in the name of ending hunger also provides some small boost to growers. As part of our overall trade strategy it discourages imports of many food products. It is ultimately a big part of our regional politics, one of many schemes used to direct government funds away from one voter constituency and toward another. Confused about even what it hopes to achieve, our farm policy is rife with contradictions, often at war with itself, consistently inconsistent.

This study traces the interesting, methodical accretion of government interference in agriculture over the last 50 years and more. It looks closely at such auxiliary farm programs as the farm credit system, the food stamp program, the protections for dairymen and sugar growers. And it examines in detail the efficiency of federal farm policy in improving the well-being of low-income farm people.

# Acknowledgments

In preparing this manuscript for publication I have benefited from criticism and suggestions by Gary Santoni, a former colleague at the Federal Reserve Bank of St. Louis, and by Professors Charles Orvis at Rhodes College, Dail Bails at Memphis State University, and E. C. Pasour at North Carolina State University. None bears any responsibility for errors, omissions, or viewpoints in the final product, however. I am especially grateful for the assistance provided by the Government Documents Section of Memphis State University Library. Saundra Williams and her staff were most helpful in obtaining hard-to-find materials and documents. In addition, I want to express my gratitude to Doris Johnson for performing the secretarial work, making obvious corrections, and assuming the burden of keeping the various parts of the study in order. Finally, I want to thank Karl Zinsmeister for his yeoman efforts in editing the manuscript and making it—I hope—readable for laymen as well as agricultural economists.

# 1. Birth of the Farm Programs

Prior to World War I there was little direct federal support for farming in this country. What programs existed were peripheral efforts to expand markets, reduce monopolies, and increase the supply of credit and farm supplies. Specifically, the government supported farm cooperatives, credit unions, and farmer education. There was no government intervention in markets to increase commodity prices and farm incomes. Prices and incomes were determined entirely by supply and demand conditions, and individual farmers made production decisions based on price signals.

## The Origin of Price Supports

As early as the late 19th century, complaints were raised about the uneven fates farmers faced in an open marketplace, and pleas were heard for federal intervention. In 1894, the National Grange (a major farm organization) endorsed David Lubin's proposal for an export subsidy on agricultural staples to be financed by the federal government. In June of that year, Lubin got the proposal adopted by the Republican State Convention of California as a plank in its platform. In 1895, an export bounty bill was introduced in Congress (Taylor 1952, 12–15). Its stated objective was "to restore to the producer of staple agricultural products his purchasing power by assisting him to meet his unequal competition." Lubin argued that while farmers' products had to be sold at world free-trade prices, U.S. manufacturers were able to sell their output in a protected domestic market at relatively high prices. And it was predominantly farmers who paid the tariff duties on imported items. Consequently, he insisted, farmers suffer an economic injustice. Prior to getting his bill introduced in Congress, Lubin encouraged two University of Michigan students to prepare papers on the proposal. Both concluded that the subsidy would *stimulate* farm production (which is opposite from the effect desired by someone who wants to increase agricultural prices). Nevertheless, Lubin

1

continued to fight for the bounty, and it was defeated twice in the late 1890s (Taylor 1952, 16–18).

After the turn of the century, political pressure for direct government assistance to agriculture subsided somewhat because of relatively favorable price relationships, which continued through World War I. But the sharp decline in farm commodity prices following World War I resulted in renewed agitation for government support. Farm organizations became disillusioned with the prospects for achieving prosperity through cooperatives, freight rate reduction, new credit, and other indirect measures.

Throughout the early proposals for government assistance to agriculture it was argued that farmers were in an unfavorable situation relative to other members of society. Professor John D. Black of Harvard University, after reviewing the economic literature of the period, reported that "social scientists in the 1920s did not know enough about the functioning of agriculture in the national and world economy to suggest lines of remedial action that went to the root of the problems" (Black 1959, 564–65). Basic economic principles of supply and demand, marginal costs, marginal revenue, and factor adjustments in response to price changes were seldom considered in discussions of the proposed programs. Occasionally there was recognition of the fact that raising farm commodity prices would provide incentives for farmers to increase production, but the implications of that fact were not well thought through.

A major thesis of proponents of government price supports was that market forces affected the country's farm and nonfarm sectors unequally, indeed that market forces might not be appropriate for governing a farm economy. The argument was stated by Alexander Legge, chairman of the Federal Farm Board, at the American Farm Economics Association meeting in Washington, D.C., in December 1929: "Industry must in order to live, regulate from day to day the flow of its product to what the consuming demand may be . . . while in agriculture each fellow, 6,000,000 of them, goes all by himself regardless of what the consuming demand may be" (Legge 1930, 6).[1] Professor John G. Thompson refused to accept the idea

[1]Prior to his appointment as chairman of the Federal Farm Board (a new federal corporation designed to stabilize farm commodity prices), Alexander Legge was president of International Harvester Company, one of the nation's major farm machinery manufacturers.

2

that workers left agriculture because of declining returns (Thompson 1922). E. G. Nourse, later the first chairman of the President's Council of Economic Advisers, likewise saw no hope in 1927 for a prosperous market-based agriculture[2] (Nourse 1927). The view that agriculture was not subject to the same basic economic forces as other industries and would not adjust sufficiently to unfavorable prices to equalize farmers' incomes with those of other American workers became the prevailing view not only of farm leaders and farm organizations but also of leading farm economists of the period. In fact, this view became so generally accepted that in the mid-1920s both houses of Congress and later the Hoover administration took action based on its premise.

Following World War I, legislative proposals for federal intervention in farm commodity markets unfolded at an accelerated pace. The Norris Bill, originally introduced in 1915, reintroduced in the early 1920s and supported by leading farm organizations, including the Farmers National Council, proposed a $100 million government corporation to purchase U.S. farm products for cash and sell them abroad on credit over a period of five years. Though supported by elected representatives from the farm states, it was eventually set aside. In the winter of 1923–24 it was revised as the Norris-Sinclair Bill, which authorized establishment of a government corporation to purchase U.S. farm products and sell them abroad for foreign securities, the securities to be sold to American investors (Benedict 1953, 207–8). A measure providing for outright government price fixing of farm products, the Christopherson Bill was the subject of extensive hearings by the House Committee on Agriculture in 1922. It authorized the government to establish a price for each major farm product, buying up any surplus not sold at the fixed price. No provision was made for the disposal of products acquired in the price-fixing operations (Benedict 1953, 207).

Other legislative efforts to obtain direct price supports for farm

[2]Edwin G. Nourse was one of the most influential farm economists of this period, a frequent contributor of articles to professional journals, and a participant in numerous farm problem study groups. Hence, when the Council of Economic Advisers was established in 1946 to provide economic advice and analysis to the president, Nourse was selected as its first chairman. He resigned in 1949 because of his conviction that the council should maintain a professional posture as distinguished from executive policymaking and political affairs.

products considered during the early 1920s included the Ladd-Sinclair, Gooding, and Little bills. The Ladd-Sinclair Bill authorized a U.S. government corporation to purchase sufficient quantities of farm products to assure prices that would cover production costs plus a reasonable profit. The commodities acquired in such operations could be sold to domestic customers or foreign buyers at prices the corporation deemed advisable. Hence, it was essentially an export subsidy measure for which an appropriation of $1 billion was authorized. The Gooding Bill authorized the creation of a $300 million government corporation to purchase wheat at fixed prices during the three years 1923–25. The corporation could then sell the wheat at such prices as it deemed best for public welfare. The Little Bill provided $30 million for the secretary of agriculture to purchase and store wheat, with additional treasury certificates to be issued after 25 million bushels had been stored. The purchases were to be made at $1.40 to $1.50 per bushel if wheat dropped below that level, and the secretary was directed to sell it whenever the price reached $1.85 per bushel in New York and Chicago (Benedict 1953, 208).

## McNary-Haugenism: A Two-Price Plan Emerges

Outside Congress there were other proposals for "restoring the purchasing power of farmers." Following the National Agricultural Conference of 1922, George N. Peek and Hugh S. Johnson of the Moline Plow Company prepared a statement for private circulation that ultimately became the basis for much of the New Deal agricultural legislation of 1933. The Peek-Johnson proposal entitled *Equality for Agriculture* called for a government corporation that would essentially maintain two prices for agricultural products. Domestic prices would be maintained well above market levels, and crops not consumed domestically would be sold abroad at prevailing world prices. The desired domestic price levels would be attained by government purchases of surplus products (Benedict 1953, 208–9).

Secretary of Agriculture Henry C. Wallace became interested in the proposal and initiated a series of studies in the Department of Agriculture to test the possibilities of the plan. The secretary became increasingly disposed toward implementing the plan, but with the death of President Harding in 1923 and the inauguration of President Coolidge, the administration's interest in farm income supports took a sharp decline. The new president was a fervent proponent of market-based solutions to most economic problems.

Despite this unfavorable turn in political support, Secretary Wallace, with the energetic cooperation of Peek and Johnson, continued to work for approval of the plan. He used the Wheat Growers Association as a vehicle for selling the idea. The association's efforts, aided by bankers and others in the Pacific Northwest, led to the rise of a number of other lobbies pressing for government price fixing and agricultural marketing (Benedict 1953, 210–11).

With the secretary's encouragement, USDA staff members drafted legislation incorporating the Peek-Johnson proposals in a bill introduced in both houses in 1924 as the McNary-Haugen Act. This bill (five versions were eventually introduced) was the centerpiece of proposed farm legislation throughout the second half of the 1920s.

As in the original Peek-Johnson plan, the proposal called for a two-price system—domestic and foreign—for specified farm products, aiming to obtain a higher average price for all farm output. This separation of the market was to be achieved by a government corporation that would increase domestic food prices and push exports (Benedict 1953, 211–14). Proponents of the plan recognized that tariffs on agricultural imports would have to be raised or else purchasers of farm products would just switch to foreign suppliers.

While early support for the program was mainly in the wheat states, Secretary Wallace proselytized widely on its behalf. Despite opposition within the Coolidge administration, he made speeches throughout the nation to the effect that USDA consideration was being given to boosting farmers' income. The first McNary-Haugen Bill was defeated in the House in 1924. Peek established himself in Washington and led the fight for the second McNary-Haugen Bill in 1925, but it did not come to a vote.

The third McNary-Haugen Bill was introduced with some changes in both the House and Senate in 1926 but was defeated in both chambers. A fourth McNary-Haugen Bill, which included price supports for wheat, cotton, rice, corn, and hogs, was reported out of the House and Senate committees in 1927 and finally passed by both houses with the support of Vice President Dawes. President Coolidge, however, vetoed the bill. The vigorous veto message contended that the bill would not aid farmers as a whole and that the fee charged to finance the program would employ the coercive

5

powers of the government against the many for the benefit of the few (Benedict 1953, 220–28).

A fifth McNary-Haugen Bill, passed in 1928 by large majorities in both houses, was likewise vetoed, and the veto was again sustained. However, as pointed out by Henry C. Taylor, the founder of agricultural economics, the view was emerging that the price of farm products as determined by supply and demand might not be a "fair" price. This type of thinking continued to make headway among farm organizations and in the political arena, leading for the first time to creation of a federal agency for supporting farm prices during the Hoover administration (Taylor 1952, 509).[3]

## The Triumph of Price Supports:
## Creation of the Federal Farm Board

As indicated by Congress's repeated passage of the McNary-Haugen bills, the only brake on federal farm price support legislation in the late 1920s was the president. And in the 1928 presidential campaign, both candidates promised to call a special session of Congress to enact agricultural relief. Consequently, from the election of President Hoover came the Agricultural Marketing Act of 1929, creating the Federal Farm Board.

This act called for government assistance in four courses of action:
(1) Minimizing speculation,
(2) Preventing inefficient and wasteful methods of distribution,
(3) Encouraging the organization of producers into effective marketing associations, and,
(4) Aiding in preventing and controlling surpluses in any agricultural commodity so as to prevent undue fluctuations or depressions in prices.

For carrying out these broad policies the president, with the advice and consent of the Senate, was authorized to appoint a board of eight members, consisting of representatives of farm suppliers and producers of major agricultural commodities. Included among its original members was the president of the International Harvester Company as chairman, along with representatives of tobacco, grain, dairy, citrus, cotton, and fruit producers, plus the secretary

[3]For an excellent discussion of the numerous proposals of government price supports in the 1920s, which eventually resulted in the massive domestic farm programs, see Hadwiger 1970, chapters 4 and 5.

of agriculture as an ex officio member. The board was provided a revolving fund of $500 million for carrying out the functions specified in the Agricultural Marketing Act.[4]

The fund was to be used as a special banking facility for farm cooperatives, making loans to them at more favorable terms than could be obtained from commercial banks or other private agencies. The board was authorized to make loans to cooperatives for merchandising; construction of marketing, processing, and storing facilities; membership expansions; and credit advances to growers.

In addition, the board was authorized to set up stabilization corporations for controlling "surpluses" that might arise. Loans could be made to these corporations out of the revolving fund and if earnings from the stabilization operations were insufficient to repay the loan, the loss could be absorbed out of the fund (U.S. *Statutes at Large*, 46:11).

### Commodity Market Intervention

The Federal Farm Board undertook its assigned task in mid-1929 on the eve of the Great Depression.[5] Within a few months the nation's most devastating stock market crash occurred, and during the next three years farm commodity prices declined 57 percent.

An early objective of the board was to use large farm cooperative associations to carry out price stabilization. Major associations created by the board for this purpose included the American Cotton Cooperative Association, the Farmers National Grain Corporation, the National Wool Marketing Corporation, the National Bean Marketing Association, the National Livestock Marketing Association, the National Pecan Marketing Association, the National Beet Growers Association, and the National Fruit and Vegetable Exchange.

As the depression unfolded in the fall of 1929, the newly created board mounted numerous efforts to stem the sharp price declines of most farm commodities. It looked upon the price declines as a temporary slump and felt justified in attempting to counter them by massive purchases until the expected recovery occurred.

[4]This amount, while relatively small compared with federal budgets today, amounted to 16 percent of annual federal outlays at the time and about 2.5 times the operating budget of the U.S. Department of Agriculture.

[5]For an excellent discussion of the cause of the Great Depression see Meltzer 1976, 459–61.

In late 1929 the board began to offer loans at concessionary rates to cooperatives, accepting as collateral the commodities purchased by the cooperatives from their member farmers. The specific actions taken and the outcome of these operations can be illustrated by a brief discussion of a few of the individual programs, especially those of wheat and cotton, which were the most expensive (Benedict 1953, 256–66; Hadwiger 1970, 110–12).

The Federal Farm Board's fiasco with wheat began with a call to farmers to slow up deliveries to markets in late 1929 and the offer of favorable loan terms to wheat cooperatives, the loans secured by stored wheat. By May 1930 the Farm Board and the Farmers National Grain Corporation together held over 65 million bushels of wheat, 10 percent of annual production. Prices continued to weaken as the depression deepened and the board's accumulations of wheat through price supporting actions accelerated. At mid–1931, the board held 231 million bushels or 25 percent of annual production and decided to drop its price support operations, adopting a policy of liquidating its holdings so as to avoid adverse effects on world markets if possible. On the favorable side, farmers are estimated to have received 20 to 25 cents per bushel more for wheat during the period of the board's price support operations. But as the purchases stopped, the price of wheat dropped sharply.

Liquidation of the surplus wheat stocks by the board was largely on a concessional basis, with sizable sales to Germany and China for long-term bonds and some bartered to Brazil for coffee. The remaining stocks were liquidated in 1932 and 1933 at major losses. Total losses by the board on wheat stabilization probably exceeded $150 million, or one-third of its entire revolving fund (Benedict 1953, 261–62).

The board's cotton price stabilization program was similar to the one for wheat. Concessionary loans were granted to farm cooperatives, using their cotton as collateral. When the board bailed out the cooperatives by taking over the cotton, its market value was well below the amount of the loan outstanding. Through its Cotton Stabilization Corporation, the board took over 1.3 million cotton bales in 1930, about 10 percent of the previous year's crop, worth more than $107.5 million. By August 1932, the board and the cooperatives held 3.5 million bales, or about 25 percent of annual production. In May the board had decided to stop further advances to the cotton cooperatives as almost all its funds were committed to wheat and cotton. It further announced that liquidations of its cotton holdings would begin in August with sales limited to about 650,000 bales per year. Cotton prices leveled off somewhat in 1932 as a result of a 4-million-bale decline in production from 1931, easing somewhat the board's stabilization operations. Nevertheless, its losses on cotton operations still totaled about $50 million or 10 percent of the revolving fund (Benedict 1953, 259–60; Benedict 1955, 117).

In addition to wheat and cotton, the board made specific efforts to stabilize the prices of butter, grapes, and wool. Expenditures in these areas, however, were relatively small, and outstanding balances near the close of the board's operations in 1933 totaled only $11.5, $16.9, and $16.2 million for the dairy, fruit and vegetable, and wool cooperatives, respectively (Benedict 1955, 108).

### The Failure of Price Supports

The Farm Board's efforts to prevent farm commodity price declines during the early 1930s ultimately only delayed the slide a short while. During its operation, massive quantities of commodities were held off the market through subsidized loans or purchases at above-market prices. The board's losses during the period of price supporting activities, 1928–33, totaled at least two-thirds of the revolving fund. About 50 percent of the loss was from wheat operations, 15 to 20 percent from cotton, and the remainder from dairy, grapes, and wool.[6]

Outside a period of general economic decline, the board's performance might have been better, but given the complicated information required to outperform private markets, it is unlikely any public agency could succeed at its task.

### Summary

This chapter has discussed federal government activities in agriculture prior to the massive New Deal programs of the early 1930s. Initially, government support was indirect: increasing farm credit, supporting cooperatives, expanding farmer education, and so forth.

---

[6]The Federal Farm Board was abolished in 1933, and its assets were transferred to the Farm Credit Administration.

As a result of growing feeling among farmers and some politicians that agriculture was ill-treated in a competitive economy, pressure grew during the 1920s for government efforts to assure farmers "equality of income" with the rest of the economy.

When farm prices declined after World War I, the arguments for government intervention became more sophisticated. It was said that, unlike industrial production, agriculture does not adjust or adjusts very slowly to changing economic conditions. Consequently, a decline in export demand or an increase in supply through improved technology sharply worsens the condition of farms, with no self-adjustment mechanism available. As a result, government intervention to stabilize farm prices and increase farmers' income was said to be essential.

As in the national tariff controversies, the middle- and long-term effects of federal intervention on the national economy, on farm incentives, and on individual well-being were not well thought out. Advocates of federal farm subsidies ignored evidence that they would only exacerbate the deepest problem of American agriculture—chronic overproduction, which could only be cured by structural migration of farmers into other occupations.

In an attempt to bolster farm incomes and keep them competitive with other occupations, numerous bills were introduced in Congress in the 1920s. Most of them involved a two-price plan for most agricultural products—one artificially inflated by government regulation for domestic users, and a lower world-market price for output sold abroad. Increasing support for such legislation developed in Congress during the course of the decade, and only strong executive branch opposition prevented direct price supports from being instituted during the Coolidge administration, ending in early 1929.

Both political parties promised federal assistance for agriculture during the 1928 election campaign. Following President Hoover's inauguration, the Federal Farm Board, provided with a massive revolving fund, was created to directly support farm prices. The board had no authority to control production, and as domestic prices of some major crops were raised above world prices by its actions, the board accumulated large surplus stocks of farm products. Some short-term gains to farmers occurred as the nation drifted into the Great Depression. Over the longer run, however, the price supports were a fiasco. They caused a reduction in exports of wheat and cotton, provided farmers incentive for increased production, while massive government-purchased stocks accumulated in warehouses at great cost to taxpayers and consumers. Finally, the board's funds were depleted in the early 1930s and its stocks of commodities liquidated at much lower prices, worsening an already severely depressed farm commodity market.

# 2. A New Deal for Agriculture Emerges

Following the election of President Franklin D. Roosevelt in 1932 and the sweeping victory of the Democratic party, political pressure became overwhelming for programs to implement the New Deal, the main theme of the election campaign. Efforts to alleviate the distress of the farm sector were high on the list of the new administration's objectives. For this purpose the president appointed as secretary of agriculture Henry A. Wallace, a farm journal editor. Wallace was an avid convert to Thorstein Veblen's institutional economic views and believed that the great productive capacity of American industry was deliberately being curtailed by selfish businessmen for personal profit to the detriment of the farmer (Schapsmeier 1968, 32).[1]

The nation was in the throes of the Great Depression, and agriculture was in even greater distress than the rest of the economy, reflecting major export losses resulting from the recently enacted high tariff barriers. The average price received by farmers for products sold had declined 57 percent over the three years 1929–32, and net farm income plummeted further than prices. Farm foreclosures and bankruptcies were rampant. Rural banks and other farm lenders were searching for any available means to avoid bankruptcy themselves. Hence, a major task of government as seen by the elected representatives was to enact emergency farm programs that would provide immediate relief.

## The Birth of "Parity"

The Agricultural Adjustment Act, creating the Agricultural Adjustment Administration (AAA), was one of the earliest legislative

---

[1]Wallace shared with Veblen the view that wealthy capitalists of the nation reveling in conspicuous consumption deliberately curtailed the enormous productive capacity of the nation in order to enhance their personal profit. This outlook explained for him why the economic system favored financiers and bankers and provided sufficient reason for the inauguration of a planned farm production program under government direction (Schapsmeier 1968, 34–36).

actions taken by the new Congress. It was approved by the president in May 1933. Its stated objective was "to relieve the existing national economic emergency by increasing agricultural purchasing power, to raise revenue for extraordinary expenses incurred by reason of such emergency, to provide emergency relief with respect to agricultural indebtedness, to provide for the orderly liquidation of joint-stock land banks, and for other purposes" (U.S. *Statutes at Large*, 48:31).

While the Agricultural Adjustment Act provided for emergency farm mortgage relief, its main thrust was toward increasing farm incomes through price supports and production adjustments that would raise commodity prices. Though no exact support level was specified, the stated policy had three goals:

(1) To establish and maintain such balance between the production and consumption of agricultural commodities . . . as will reestablish prices to farmers at a level . . . equivalent to the purchasing power of agricultural commodities in the base period. The base period in the case of all agricultural commodities except tobacco shall be the prewar period, August 1909–July 1914. In the case of tobacco, the base period shall be the postwar period, August 1919–July 1929.

(2) To approach such equality of purchasing power by gradual correction of the present inequalities therein at as rapid a rate as is deemed feasible in view of the current consumptive demand in domestic and foreign markets.

(3) To protect the consumers' interest by readjusting farm production at such level as will not increase the percentage of the consumers' retail expenditures for agricultural commodities, or products derived therefrom, . . . above the percentage which was returned to the farmer in the prewar period, August 1909–July 1914 (U.S. *Statutes at Large*, 48:32).

What came to be defined as "parity" required that farm products be priced such that a given quantity sold would provide income sufficient to purchase the same amount of nonfarm products as during the base period.

The methods authorized for achieving the price increases and higher income objectives were diverse and not very precise. The Agricultural Adjustment Act authorized the secretary of agriculture "to reduce acreage or production for market of any 'basic' agricultural commodity through voluntary agreements with producers, or by other voluntary methods." He could make rental or benefit payments on land in such amounts as deemed "fair and reasonable" and could also make advance payments on nonperishable commodities stored and sealed on farms, under prescribed regulations. He could enter into marketing agreements with processors, associations, producers, and others for the purpose of controlling the prices paid to farmers, handlers, and processors. Each of these actions was designed to reduce the volume of farm commodities marketed.

Prices for the basic crops were guaranteed by the U.S. government by granting producers nonrecourse loans on their stored commodities held by the Commodity Credit Corporation (CCC), a government agency established in 1933 for this purpose. If prices on the commodities fell below the predetermined support level, the farmer was not required to repay his loans and had satisfied his obligation to the government by surrendering his rights to the commodity. The government incurred the realized losses. On the other hand, if the market price rose above the loan rate by a sufficient amount to cover storage and interest costs, the farmer could exercise his right to withdraw the commodity from storage, pay the storage and interest costs, and sell at the market price, realizing the profit.

The basic agricultural commodities included in the original act were wheat, cotton, field corn, hogs, rice, tobacco, and milk and dairy products. Others were added in succeeding years as new acts and amendments relative to this basic legislation were passed. In order to obtain the revenue for financing the program, the secretary was given authority to levy processing taxes on farm products up to the amount of "the difference between the current average farm price of the commodity and its 'fair' exchange value." This was the principal method of financing the rental and benefit payments prior to the Supreme Court's decision nullifying the act in 1936.[2] An

[2] In January 1936 the Supreme Court declared unconstitutional the processing taxes levied on cotton for the purpose of financing the act and further held that the Constitution did not grant the federal government power to regulate agricultural production within the states. This deprived the Department of Agriculture of its principal source of financing and at the same time made invalid all the contracts and agreements made with individual growers for reducing production. The administration and Congress immediately enacted the Soil Conservation and Domestic Allotment Act, which authorized direct appropriations to finance the program and

appropriation of $100 million was made for administrative expenses and to finance the program in its initial stages. Following the Court decision in 1936, the Soil Conservation and Domestic Allotment Act was passed, which retained most features of the original act but dropped the processing tax. The program was then financed by direct appropriations from the U.S. Treasury.

The sugar program established under the Jones-Costigan Act of 1934, to be discussed in greater detail in chapter 10, was somewhat different from other crop programs. Almost 50 percent of sugar consumed in the United States was imported; hence, the price to domestic producers could be set at almost any desired level through tariffs and import quotas. Prior to Jones-Costigan, domestic sugar producers were favored by a tariff on imports. Since then, quotas have been employed, distributed arbitrarily to the various nations exporting sugar to the United States in amounts just sufficient to assure that the predetermined price is received by domestic producers. Thus price supports for sugar are not a heavy burden to taxpayers as most of the cost is borne through the artificially higher prices charged domestic consumers.

With the exception of dairy products and wool, supply controls and price supports on livestock products have been limited to short periods and have never been very effective. At the beginning of AAA activities, brood sows and pigs were purchased by the government at premium prices and slaughtered in order to reduce the amount of pork marketed. As a large fraction of the population was short of food during the trough of the depression, the public reacted strongly against this program and it was soon discontinued. In succeeding years the government occasionally made sizable purchases of livestock or livestock products during periods of sharp price declines, but the AAA made little effort to reduce production of meat animals. What meat was purchased was distributed to low-income families, to schools for lunch programs, or for similar purposes.

The dairy programs, discussed in more detail in chapter 9, were extremely controversial from the beginning. Costs of milk, cheese, butter, and so forth were highly observable, and efforts to raise

---

direct payments for taking land out of soil-depleting crops and planting it in soil-conserving crops. It was a milder program than the preceding one but essentially accomplished the same purpose.

prices met with strong opposition from distributors and consumers. In the beginning, marketing agreements were made to govern prices. Supply was also restricted by setting quality standards, establishing quotas for individual farmers, and occasionally purchasing dairy cows for slaughter. Since 1949, milk prices have been supported directly by the federal government through the purchase of all milk that cannot be sold to consumers at the federally established support price.

Federal aid to wool producers has been handled in a way similar to sugar, as a large percentage of domestic wool consumption is imported. Prior to World War II, wool prices were elevated through trade barriers. Following the war, with the presssure to open up international trade, operations were shifted toward direct government subsidies to domestic wool producers. A continued barrier to imports was thus masked in the price system, as the subsidy led to greater domestic production than would have occurred without it, and little relief to trade resulted.

## Reducing Production

The secretary of agriculture's report to the president on December 12, 1934, following the first full year of the New Deal farm programs, outlined the initial efforts:

> Naturally the first steps involved reducing production. In 1933 agriculture had enormous surpluses of wheat, cotton, tobacco, and hog products, which had accumulated as a result of wartime expansion, economic nationalism, strangled foreign trade, the disappearance of foreign markets, and reduced domestic consumption. Prices had fallen far below costs. Merely to avert farm ruin, it was imperative to eliminate the surpluses.

Two methods were used toward that end: acreage controls and marketing agreements that restricted the quantities farmers could grow.

At one point in the report, Secretary Wallace stated:

> It was never contemplated that reduction, once started, should be continued indefinitely. . . . It would be a serious mistake to reduce farm production constantly. Such a course would raise prices temporarily, but would restrict consumption, and create new farm competition at home and abroad.

Nonetheless, elsewhere in the report the secretary argued for permanent controls:

> Essentially, agriculture needs production control to prevent the mass swings that lead to recurring cycles of over and under production. Adopted as an emergency device, a means for averting irremediable disaster . . . the control principle has nevertheless permanent as well as emergency uses. . . . Recurring cycles in production blocked steady farm prosperity; adjustment to demand through blind competition caused farmers to rush in and out of different enterprises. Whenever any crop showed a profit, producers grew more until the profit had been stamped into the ground. . . . without means of coordinating their production, farmers could not for long keep a satisfactory balance between production and consumption (U.S. Department of Agriculture 1935, 1–3, 28–29).

## Underway with the AAA

In pursuit of its objective of increasing the purchasing power of farmers as quickly as possible, the AAA immediately initiated a program of supply controls and price supports for the basic crops listed in the Agricultural Adjustment Act. By the time the administrative organization was in place in 1933, most crops had already been planted. But the desire to reduce supplies was so urgent that growers were offered payments to plow up growing crops and to slaughter young pigs and pregnant sows. By 1934, longer-range programs had been developed for reducing the acreage planted on each farm through allotments based on the acreage of the crop grown during the base period.

While the programs varied from one commodity to another, those for crops generally included a rental payment for land that farmers agreed to take out of production and a price guarantee for crops grown on the reduced (allotted) acres. Acreages were allotted to each farm by local committees in each county or township, usually on the basis of average crop size from 1930 to 1932. Since no records were available to determine previous plantings, the allotments were based largely on the farmers' own reports.

The Soil Conservation and Domestic Allotment Act of 1936 retained most of the features of the Agricultural Adjustment Act. However, instead of making land rental payments to farmers on acres with-

18

drawn from production, it authorized payments for approved soil building practices on the withdrawn land. Also, the Soil Conservation Service was established in 1935 to assist farmers in almost every agricultural county of the nation.

In addition to its efforts to improve the well-being of farmers through supply controls and price supports, the government took action on the farm credit front. Unlike most AAA programs, which were designed to aid the agricultural industry as a whole, the early credit programs were largely welfare measures designed to aid those requiring emergency assistance. They authorized federal government credit to refinance farm mortgages, reduce interest rates on existing bank loans, and refinance irrigation and other agricultural improvement districts. Credit to farmers was further liberalized in 1937 under the Bankhead-Jones Farm Tenancy Act, which set up the Farm Security Administration (later the Farmers Home Administration or FmHA). It provided tenants, croppers, and farm laborers with loans to purchase farms, at up to 100 percent of the value of the land, equipment, and capital requirements, all at subsidized interest rates, with payments amortized at up to 40 years. As will be discussed in chapter 8, this program was greatly liberalized and expanded over the years to include nearly all farmers and almost any request for farm credit.

## Summary

Aid to agriculture was given high priority in the New Deal at the nadir of the Great Depression. Congress quickly enacted the Agricultural Adjustment Act, which was largely based on the earlier price support and supply control proposals contained in the McNary-Haugen bills. This act and later legislation also included features to alleviate individual hardships in agriculture, such as temporary mortgage relief and easier credit terms for low-income farmers.

These programs represented a new policy of government intervention in the business affairs of individual farmers. They marked the turning point from a free to a highly controlled farm economy. The major emphasis of the new regimen was on supply reduction, through acreage controls for basic crops or, in the case of dairy products and fresh produce, through price supports and marketing agreements. Confusion entered the process when special programs were added to enhance soil conservation and alleviate poverty in agriculture. Direct assistance to less affluent farmers through credit and managerial services worked counter to the acreage reduction programs in that they tended to increase resources in agriculture and enhance supply. Farm programs thus operated at cross purposes, and the impact of higher prices on domestic demand and exports was largely ignored.

# 3. The First Phase: Supply Management

The first phase of the Agricultural Adjustment Act programs extended from 1933 into the mid-1950s. It began with emergency depression-era measures. Then World War II led to a spurt in demand for U.S. farm products and sharp increases in prices. Price ceilings were placed on most farm products during the later war years, but guaranteed price supports also climbed throughout the war, allegedly to assure enhanced production.

Following World War II, supply and demand for farm products were just returning to normal levels when the Korean War led to another sharp increase in commodity prices, delaying until 1952 their return to normal levels. The wartime ceilings had been eliminated, but high price supports were maintained. High food prices tended to increase production and reduce the quantity of farm commodities demanded. Consequently, a buildup of commodity surpluses occurred in three waves of increasing intensity: the first prior to World War II, the second following the war, and the third following the Korean War. The buildups occurred despite attempts to restrain output through acreage controls.

## Soaring Yields

The impact of the New Deal farm programs on production in their first four years, 1934–37, is difficult to assess. It is clear, however, that some reduction in output did occur. As indicated in Table 3.1, total acres of crops harvested were down 8.7 percent, and acreage of the major controlled crops (corn, wheat, cotton, and tobacco) declined even more sharply. Corn planting dropped 20 percent, from an average of 91.5 million acres during the years 1930–33 (prior to the programs) to 73.2 million acres in the four years following. Wheat acreage was down 9 percent, cotton 20 percent, and tobacco 18 percent. These data indicate that, with the possible exception of wheat, the acreage reduction program was effective in reducing production.

21

## Table 3.1

### ACREAGE, YIELD, AND PRODUCTION OF SELECTED CROPS BEFORE AND AFTER AAA

| Crop | 1930–33 | | | 1934–37 | | |
|---|---|---|---|---|---|---|
| | Acres (Millions) | Yield | Production (Millions) | Acres (Millions) | Yield | Production (Millions) |
| Corn (for grain) | 91.5 | 23.7 bu. | 2,168 bu. | 73.2 | 23.1 bu. | 1,689 bu. |
| Oats | 39.6 | 27.7 bu. | 1,098 bu. | 34.7 | 26.8 bu. | 931 bu. |
| Wheat | 56.9 | 13.8 bu. | 784 bu. | 52.0 | 12.8 bu. | 665 bu. |
| Rice (rough) | 0.90 | 2,110 lb. | 19 cwt. | 0.93 | 2,194 lb. | 20.4 cwt. |
| Cotton | 36.6 | 195 lb. | 14.3 bales | 29.4 | 219 lb. | 12.9 bales |
| Soybeans | 1.1 | 13.6 bu. | 15 bu. | 2.4 | 15.8 bu. | 38 bu. |
| Tobacco | 1.81 | 774 lb. | 1,401 lb. | 1.48 | 865 lb. | 1,280 lb. |
| All Crops | 361.25 | — | — | 329.75 | — | — |

SOURCE: U.S. Department of Agriculture, *Agricultural Statistics, 1972*; and *Economic Indicators of the Farm Sector: Production and Efficiency Statistics, 1981*.

Part of the reduction, however, was caused by unusually severe droughts during two or three years, which affected both crop acres and yields. It is difficult to tell how much of the production decline was actually program-inspired. It is known, however, that during these early years farmers were sluggish in responding to the new federal incentives. For instance, the desired effects of the acreage restrictions were often circumvented because farmers simply changed cropping patterns rather than actually withdrawing land from use.

By the late 1930s and early 1940s, farmers were responding to the acreage controls and higher price incentives through changing patterns of production. They were becoming skilled at making acreage reductions to comply with the restrictions, then intensifying their tillage, so the overall effect of the controls on farming operations was minimized.

Annual rates of change in farm productivity from the 1920s through the early 1950s, as shown in Table 3.2, indicate farmers' response to the new price incentives and supply management efforts. First, note that the acreage controls, while reducing the amount of land planted for most controlled crops except wheat, apparently had little effect on total crop acres planted. Total acres remained unchanged in the ten years from 1922–23 to 1932–33 and declined only about 1 percent during each of the two decades following. Clearly, noncontrolled crops were substituted for controlled ones, so overall tillage took place on about the same number of acres.

While total crop acres were stable, yields rose sharply, reflecting the rising incentive to produce. Overall crop yields had declined 0.4 percent per year in the pre-program decade but rose at annual rates of 2.4 percent and 0.8 percent respectively during the first two decades of the programs—a total increase of 26 percent in the first decade and 7 percent in the second. Average yields of each major crop under the acreage control program rose faster than the average for other crops. With higher prices in prospect, farmers substituted other inputs for land. Land devoted to corn was reduced 1.6 percent per year from 1932–33 to 1942–43, but yields increased 3.2 percent annually. Though corn acreage was reduced further during the following decade, yields continued to increase 2 percent per year, so production rose sharply nonetheless.

While acreage restrictions were less severe for wheat, some reduction was achieved (0.6 percent per year) and yield increases

*Table 3.2*

ANNUAL RATES OF CHANGE IN ACREAGE, YIELD, AND
PRODUCTION OF SELECTED CROPS (%)

| Crop | 1922–23 to 1932–33 | 1932–33 to 1942–43 | 1942–43 to 1952–53 |
|---|---|---|---|
| Corn (for grain) | | | |
| Acres | 1.2 | −1.6 | −1.3 |
| Yield | −1.1 | 3.2 | 2.0 |
| Production | 0 | 1.6 | 0.7 |
| Oats | | | |
| Acres | −0.3 | −0.1 | −0.3 |
| Yield | −1.4 | 2.4 | −0.1 |
| Production | −1.7 | 2.2 | −0.5 |
| Wheat | | | |
| Acres | −1.1 | −0.6 | 3.2 |
| Yield | −1.1 | 3.9 | −0.1 |
| Production | −2.0 | 3.3 | 3.2 |
| Rice | | | |
| Acres | −1.3 | 5.7 | 3.6 |
| Yield | 1.9 | −0.6 | 2.0 |
| Production | 0.5 | 5.1 | 5.6 |
| Cotton | | | |
| Acres | −0.3 | −3.8 | 1.3 |
| Yield | 2.9 | 3.2 | 1.4 |
| Production | 2.7 | −0.7 | 2.7 |
| Soybeans | | | |
| Acres | — | 26.0 | 3.8 |
| Yield | — | 2.9 | 0.4 |
| Production | — | 29.4 | 4.2 |
| Tobacco | | | |
| Acres | −1.0 | −1.0 | 1.8 |
| Yield | −0.5 | 2.7 | 2.5 |
| Production | −1.3 | 1.8 | 4.4 |
| All crops | | | |
| Acres | 0 | −0.1 | −0.1 |
| Yield | −0.4 | 2.4 | 0.8 |
| Production | −0.1 | 2.2 | 0.9 |
| Feed grain production | 0 | 1.9 | 0.1 |
| Food grain production | −2.2 | 3.4 | 3.0 |
| Sugar production | 2.5 | 0 | 0 |
| Oil crop production | 3.2 | 15.4 | 1.2 |

SOURCES: U.S. Department of Agriculture, *Agricultural Statistics*, 1934, 1972, and 1983; and *Economic Indicators of the Farm Sector: Production and Efficiency Statistics*, 1981 and 1984.

were sizable (3.9 percent per year) during the first decade of the programs. During the second decade, wheat acreage actually went up, and yields declined slightly from the record highs of the early 1940s. Overall, wheat production rose sharply during the first two decades of the programs, a total of over 3 percent per year. Output of total food grains, largely wheat, almost doubled in those twenty years.

Early AAA objectives came closer to being achieved for cotton than for the other controlled crops. Acreage controls were more restrictive, because cotton producers were more willing to accept them. Acres harvested were reduced sharply—3.8 percent per year— during the first decade of the restrictions. While yields increased at a high rate—3.2 percent per year—production was still down at the end of the decade. But both acres and yield were up somewhat during the second decade of the programs, 1942–43 to 1952–53, and production was somewhat larger than at the beginning of the programs.

Tobacco acreage controls served to reduce acreage somewhat during the first decade of the programs and to limit expansion during the second decade. Again, yields rose at a high rate, 2.7 percent per year from 1932–33 to 1942–43, and at a 2.5 percent rate in the next decade. Production rose at a moderate rate in the first decade and at a high rate during the second.

As indicated earlier, an important feature of farming operations in the early years of the programs was the jump in acreage and production of noncontrolled crops. Rice and soybeans, which were not controlled, are good examples of the switch. Rice acreage rose in excess of 5 percent annually throughout the first two decades of the programs. Soybean acreage doubled every three years during the first decade and continued up at 3.8 percent per year during the second decade.

**Crop Surpluses Mount**

By the mid-1950s, the artificially high prices for farm commodities plus other government incentives to producers had led to a tremendous buildup in surpluses held in storage by the Commodity Credit Corporation. Excessive and fast-growing carryovers of surplus CCC stocks into the new marketing season were observed for numerous price-supported crops (see Table 3.3 and appendix A-1).

25

*Table 3.3*

CCC HOLDINGS OF MAJOR COMMODITIES, OWNED PLUS
AMOUNT PLEDGED FOR PRICE SUPPORT LOANS
(AVERAGE AS OF JUNE 30)

| Commodity | 1950–51 | 1955–56 |
|---|---|---|
| Corn (million bu.) | | |
| Owned | 394 | 871 |
| Security for loan | 112 | 197 |
| Total | 506 | 1,068 |
| Percentage of production (grain) | 19 | 36 |
| Cotton (thousand bales) | | |
| Owned | 57 | 7,338 |
| Security for loan | 267 | 4,520 |
| Total | 318 | 11,858 |
| Percentage of production | 3 | 85 |
| Grain sorghum (million cwt.) | | |
| Owned | 15 | 30 |
| Security for loan | 12 | 30 |
| Total | 27 | 60 |
| Percentage of production | 14 | 50 |
| Soybeans (million bu.) | | |
| Owned | — | — |
| Security for loan | 7 | 36 |
| Total | 7 | 36 |
| Percentage of production | 2 | 9 |
| Tobacco (million lb.) | | |
| Owned | — | — |
| Security for loan | 327 | 1,065 |
| Total | 327 | 1,065 |
| Percentage of production | 15 | 49 |
| Wheat (million bu.) | | |
| Owned | 203 | 864 |
| Security for loan | 164 | 210 |
| Total | 367 | 1,074 |
| Percentage of production | 37 | 111 |
| Total investment (billion $) | 2.4 | 7.2 |

SOURCES: U.S. Department of Agriculture, *Agricultural Statistics;* and *Commodity Credit Corporation Charts: A Summary of Data through September 30, 1979,* September 1980.

For example, the CCC wheat inventory in 1955–56 averaged about 1.1 billion bushels, three times that of five years earlier and more than a year's production. Corn carryover averaged 1.1 billion bushels, more than one-third annual domestic use plus exports. Almost 12 million bales of cotton were held, in excess of a year's normal domestic use plus exports.

Not only were the surpluses embarrassing, but commercial warehouses and elevators were soon filled to capacity. Milling firms often took on storage operations and private contractors built storage space or renovated private buildings. In some cases, abandoned schoolhouses and church buildings were used for temporary storage.

Of greater concern than the more storable grain and cotton surpluses were the excessive accumulations of such perishables as dairy products, fats, and oils. By April 1954, dry milk holdings purchased in support of milk prices totaled 556 million pounds. In July of the same year the butter inventory totaled 467 million pounds.

The dairy program began in 1949 with high price supports. Secretary of Agriculture Ezra Taft Benson later reported the example of one Wyoming community that had had 38 milk producers prior to the program. These producers were able to sell only a portion of their milk at grade A prices; the remainder was sold at lower prices. Following the program, 44 producers in the same area were able to sell all their milk at the grade A level, at a higher price (Benson 1962, 256). It should be no mystery why the surplus mountains grew.

### Three Waves of Surplus Stocks

The early buildup in government holdings of farm commodities came in three waves—the 1930s into World War II, the end of the war to the outbreak of the Korean conflict, and the post-Korean wave.

The beginning of the first wave of government holdings dates back to acquisitions by the Federal Farm Board in the early 1930s. Sizable losses were taken by the board in liquidating stocks of wheat, cotton, and wool. The buildup of stocks by the CCC following the Agricultural Adjustment Act was relatively slow until the late 1930s. The value of commodities held under the program at the close of 1937 totaled only $312 million, or less than 4 percent of cash farm income from marketings that year.

Price support levels were raised, however, by the Agricultural

Adjustment Act of 1938, and larger stocks soon began to accumulate. By 1940, the value of commodities by the CCC totaled $1.2 billion, or almost 15 percent of the total cash farm income for the year. During the war years, the CCC was able to unload most of the stocks, which until then had been a matter of great concern.

Following the war, a second and much larger buildup began. Price supports, which had been kept at relatively high levels throughout the war "to encourage a high level of output," were retained afterwards "to prevent sharp price and farm income declines." The value of stocks held by the CCC in loans or inventories rose from $528 million in 1946 to $3.6 billion, or 14 percent of total cash farm income, in 1949. The situation was again fortuitously relieved by rising demand as a result of the war in Korea. Stocks declined to below the $2 billion level in December 1951.

Then the third wave of commodity buildups began in 1952, near the end of the Korean conflict. This one was greater than either of the earlier two. Furthermore, it continued unabated throughout the 1950s, despite strenuous government efforts to move the surplus commodities to consumers in both this nation and the rest of the world. Stocks rose more than fourfold from 1951 to 1955.

The third increase in government commodity inventories, which led to massive holdings during the mid-1950s, included corn, grain sorghum, barley, oats, rye, rice, cotton, wheat, tobacco, soybeans, dry milk, and butter. Despite the substantial quantities of cropland taken out of production by the government through rental agreements with farmers, price supports were sufficiently high to encourage farmers to continue to increase production.

### Government Losses Mount

Heretofore, the realized losses from government farm price supports had been minimal. The surpluses that had accumulated prior to World War II actually proved to be useful as wartime demand rose. The commodities were liquidated without loss to taxpayers during the early years of the fighting.

By the late 1940s, market prices for most supported commodities had dropped well below the support levels, and government surpluses were building up at a high rate. By 1949, the CCC owned or held loans against $2.7 billion worth of farm products. But the large losses that appeared to be in the making were forestalled by the outbreak of hostilities in Korea. In the face of rising demand, liquidation was again possible without loss to taxpayers.

No war, however, allowed easy escape from the agricultural surplus mountain that piled up following the end of fighting in Korea. The CCC controlled $5.8 billion worth of farm products in mid-1954 compared to less than $1.5 billion at the end of 1952. Despite major efforts by the new Eisenhower administration to reduce the backlog through gifts and highly subsidized exports, the surpluses continued to mount.

Direct losses from CCC price support operations became a sizable factor in the national budget in the mid-1950s. In fiscal 1954, CCC losses totaled $654 million. By mid-1955, the losses had roughly doubled from the 1954 level (Appendix Table A-2). The total cost of the programs was becoming an embarrassment to national policymakers and a drag on the U.S. economy.

U.S. Department of Agriculture expenditures, largely farm subsidies, rose from $1.2 billion or 2 percent of the federal budget in 1952 to $2.6 billion or 4 percent in 1954. USDA's budget was equivalent to 38 percent of the net income of all farm operators by 1955 (Appendix Table A-1). In addition to the federal funds devoted to the subsidies, the farm program imposed substantial costs on the economy through higher product prices. By the mid-1950s, evidence of the wastefulness of these policies led the Eisenhower administration to begin a second phase of farm programs.

**Summary**

The massive farm programs administered by the AAA were initially designed to achieve higher farm commodity prices and incomes through supply reductions and limited price supports. Crop output was to be reduced by restricting the acres planted, and in the first two or three years that program seemed to be succeeding. Much of the reduction in crop output, however, was the result of intensely dry weather in 1933 and 1934. Once weather conditions returned to more normal patterns, production of most crops rose even in the face of reduced plantings, on account of accelerating yields.

After starting out at modest levels, government-guaranteed price supports were soon set well above market prices, providing great incentive for more intensive cultivation of land. This was further encouraged by increased technical assistance, large amounts of subsidized credit, and other subsidies such as cost sharing of soil building practices. Consequently, by the late 1930s, production of most crops was sharply higher and surplus stocks had built up rapidly.

During World War II, the unwanted stocks of farm products were cleared out by enhanced demand. But support prices were also raised sharply during the war and maintained thereafter. With a return to more normal demand conditions after the war, large government surpluses once again built up quickly. Surplus stocks were reduced again during the Korean War because support prices were maintained well above market clearing levels; however, surpluses became a problem again in the early 1950s.

When the Eisenhower administration began in early 1953, it found the farm situation in turmoil, with huge surpluses of most commodities, high price supports that provided incentive for excessive production, an ineffective crop production control system, and enormous costs for consumers and taxpayers.

# 4. Why Supply Management Failed

Reasons for the Agricultural Adjustment Administration's failure to reduce farm output or to exercise much control over the supply of farm products during the first phase of the programs may be grouped under three headings: farmer ingenuity in circumventing planting restrictions, rising incentives to produce because of price supports, and the production-increasing effects of other peripheral government programs, including increased farmer education, soil conservation payments, and low-cost credit for many farmers.

**Acreage Controls Leaky**

Economic analysis indicates that acreage reductions for individual crops could reduce total crop production as envisioned by the AAA officials, if rigidly enforced. Most controls, however, are not leakproof. Farmers have incentives to take their acreage reduction on land with poorer soil. Soils are seldom uniformly fertile on any farm, and no provision was contained in the program requiring the reduced acres to be on soils of average fertility. Hence, the farmer followed his economic interest, taking the least fertile acres out of production and planting his allotted acres on land with the highest fertility.

Later, many farmers were found to be using other techniques such as the skip-row planting of cotton to defeat the purpose of the acreage restrictions. By leaving half the rows in a field unplanted, a farmer could have only one acre counted against his allotment for every two acres in the field. Farmers discovered that fields tilled that way would yield 50 percent more per row than conventionally planted fields, because their plants received more sunlight and water. Farmers also improved yields on their reduced plots by intensifying capital inputs such as chemical fertilizer, improved seed, better weed controls, and so forth.

Over the longer run, farmers found other ways of circumventing acreage restrictions. In the early years of the program, for instance, livestock, dairy, and poultry farmers who had been producing corn as feed could cooperate in the corn reduction program, receive their government checks for land rental, then plant wheat on the acreage formerly devoted to corn. Wheat, while yielding somewhat less grain than corn in the Corn Belt states, is an excellent livestock ration, and the switch could be made on many farms with little loss in total feed production. In this way, farmers who did not agree to reduce the acreage of a given crop often increased their plantings of it, thereby offsetting the reductions of those who did reduce such plantings.

Another factor that tended to bring total acres harvested back to pre-control levels was the substitution of noncontrolled crops for controlled ones. Farmers soon discovered the second most profitable alternative to the controlled crop. Among the noncontrolled crops, soybean acreage, for example, rose dramatically—from one million acres in 1932–33 to more than 10 million in 1942–43. Sharp increases likewise occurred in sorghum grain, another good substitute for corn as feed for livestock, and in rice.

## The Perverse Effects of High Price Supports

While acreage controls were only partially effective in reducing acres harvested, they were even less effective in reducing production and increasing prices of farm products. Price increases anticipated as a result of acreage reductions, coupled with government price guarantees, led farmers to increase production. At the same time, higher prices for U.S. exports provided incentives for foreign farmers to increase production and for producers of substitute products at home and abroad to expand production.

Little effort was made in the first phase of the farm programs to affect farm product prices through demand with the exception of the tariff reduction moves. Action was taken at the federal level to free up foreign trade restrictions that had closed off a sizable portion of the foreign market for U.S. farm products. Beginning with the Reciprocal Trade Agreements Act of 1934, a series of tariff reducing acts and negotiations led to major reductions in international trade barriers. This had a sizable impact on export demand for farm products in later years. Reflecting the high duties imposed by the Smoot-Hawley Tariff Act of 1930, the nation's farm exports, which totaled almost one-fourth of cash farm receipts in the 1920s, declined to less than 10 percent in 1936. This decline had a major impact on farm income; hence, actions taken to lower tariff barriers tended to increase the quantity exported. Counteracting such action, however, was the 1935 amendment to the Agricultural Adjustment Act, authorizing the president to place quotas on imports of commodities if their importation hampered the program for raising farm commodity prices.[1]

Raising prices also reduced the demand for farm products both here and abroad. Government price support levels were set using the "parity ratio" formula:

index of prices received by farmers for their products
index of prices paid by farmers for their production items

Government efforts aimed to increase this ratio to the level where it stood in the period 1910–14 (when agriculture was assumed to have been on equal footing with other industries). Congressional efforts to achieve that ratio increased agricultural prices, and there was some decline in domestic use of farm products and a sizable decline in exports as a result. Agricultural exports averaged $3.2 billion annually from 1928 to 1932, prior to the New Deal programs. In 1933–37, they amounted to $2.5 billion per year. Part of this can be credited to the price supports and part to the increased tariffs of 1930 plus the generally unfavorable economic conditions throughout the world.

---

[1]This amendment authorized the president to place quotas on imports if an investigation by the Tariff Commission found that the imports would tend to render ineffective the price support programs. It was not of great importance at the time in reducing imports, as few farm commodities except sugar and coffee were imported. It was revised and broadened in the late 1930s and was made much more stringent in a 1948 amendment that directed the president to initiate an immediate investigation by the Tariff Commission if he had reason to believe that any article or articles were being or were certain to be imported into the United States that would tend to render ineffective or materially interfere with the price support programs. If its findings indicated a need for action, the president was directed to impose tariffs and import quotas on the imported products. These restrictions were further broadened in later years, tending to wall off the U.S. market for any products competitive with domestic products under price support programs. Hence, as the price support programs were expanded to encompass a major portion of U.S. farm output, our import barriers were likewise expanded despite our professed free-trade policies (Benedict 1955, 247–48).

## Cotton Market Shrinks

The early programs were especially damaging to cotton producers since a large portion of the American cotton crop was grown for export, and there were a number of close substitutes. The rigid acreage controls applied to cotton reduced production despite farmer efforts to mitigate the program. In the three years 1935–37, production was down 3 percent from the 1931–33 pre-program level of 14.4 million bales. By 1945–47 it was down 32 percent (Table 4.1). Production has never recovered to pre-program levels.

Price supports for cotton, unlike those for most other farm products, were set well above market levels from the beginning. Following the plow-up program in 1933, price supports, through the CCC loan rate, were set at 10 cents per pound for those producers who agreed to cut back on their plantings, while the market price was about 7 cents. The support price ranged from 8 to 9 cents per pound from 1937 to 1940 when the wartime increase in cotton prices began. It was increased to 21 cents per pound in 1945 and to 31 cents in 1952 (Table 4.2). With the exception of a short period following World War II and during the Korean War, the support price was maintained well above free-market prices. Consequently, U.S.-produced cotton was priced out of the world market and to a lesser extent out of the domestic market.

*Table 4.1*

PRODUCTION AND EXPORTS OF UPLAND COTTON

| Three-year Period (Average) | Acres Planted (Millions) | Production | Exports | % of production exported |
|---|---|---|---|---|
| | | (Millions of Bales) | | |
| 1931–33 | 38.6 | 14.4 | 8.7 | 60 |
| 1935–37 | 30.7 | 14.0 | 6.0 | 43 |
| 1945–47 | 19.5 | 9.8 | 3.1 | 32 |
| 1955–57 | 16.4 | 13.0 | 5.4 | 42 |
| 1965–67 | 11.3 | 10.6 | 4.1 | 38 |
| 1975–77 | 11.5 | 11.0 | 4.5 | 41 |
| 1980–82 | 13.4 | 12.2 | 5.9 | 48 |
| 1984–85[1] | 11.4 | 13.2 | 4.1 | 31 |

SOURCE: U.S. Department of Agriculture, *Agricultural Statistics.*
[1]Two years only.

34

*Table 4.2*

GOVERNMENT SUPPORT PRICES OF SELECTED
FARM COMMODITIES
($)

| Commodity | 1935 | 1940 | 1945 | 1950 | 1952 |
|---|---|---|---|---|---|
| Corn, bu. | 0.45 | 0.61 | 1.01 | 1.47 | 1.60 |
| Cotton, upland, lb. | 0.10 | 0.09 | 0.21 | 0.28 | 0.31 |
| Peanuts, lb. | — | — | 0.07 | 0.11 | 0.13 |
| Rice, cwt. | — | — | 2.82 | 4.56 | 5.04 |
| Wheat, bu. | — | 0.64 | 1.38 | 1.99 | 2.20 |
| Tobacco, flue-cured, lb. | — | 0.15 | 0.30 | 0.45 | 0.51 |
| Grain sorghum, lb. | — | 0.54 | 1.65 | 1.87 | 2.38 |
| Soybeans, bu. | — | — | 2.04 | 2.06 | 2.56 |
| Index of prices paid 1910–14 = 100[1] | 124 | 124 | 190 | 256 | 287 |

SOURCE: U.S. Department of Agriculture, *Agricultural Statistics*, 1952 and 1956.
[1]Includes interest, taxes, and wages.

Cotton exports dropped from a pre-program average of 8.7 million bales per year in 1931–33 to 6 million in 1935–37. The decline continued during the late 1930s and 1940s to a low of 3.1 million bales per year in 1945–47. A small increase occurred in the 1950s as a result of a massive government export subsidy program, but the decline continued in the 1960s, reaching a level of only about one-half the pre-program level (Table 4.1). The proportion of U.S. cotton production exported dropped from 60 percent prior to the programs to 32 percent in 1945–47.[2]

The U.S. share of world cotton exports dropped sharply following establishment of the AAA programs. In 1930–32, prior to the programs, U.S. cotton exports accounted for 68 percent of the world

[2]When the United States raises the price of a major farm product such as cotton by acreage controls, or by CCC loans and storage operations, it leads to a number of effects. First, consumers both here and abroad will reduce their purchases of cotton products. Second, foreign production of cotton will rise as a result of the higher prices realized, further reducing U.S. exports. Third, domestic production will tend to rise, given the increased incentive to producers. Fourth, production and consumption of cotton substitutes will rise as demand for cotton substitutes here and abroad is increased.

total. The U.S. share declined to 45 percent in 1935–39 following their installation, held stable at this reduced level immediately following World War II, but declined further in the late 1950s and 1960s.[3] As shown in Table 4.3, some recovery began in the early 1970s and continued into the 1980s, but cotton exports generally remained below pre-program levels. They rose significantly in 1986 following a highly subsidized export program.

While domestic consumption of cotton rose somewhat following the programs, that of competing synthetic fibers moved sharply higher. Per capita usage of rayon and acetate more than doubled from 1933 to 1940 compared to a gain of 23 percent for cotton.

*Table 4.3*

U.S. AND WORLD EXPORTS OF COTTON
(ANNUAL AVERAGES)

| Period | United States (Millions of Bales) | Principal Exporting Nations (Millions of Bales) | U.S. Export Share (% of World Exports) |
|---|---|---|---|
| 1925–29 | 8.6 | 13.2 | 70 |
| 1930–32 | 8.2 | 12.1 | 68 |
| 1935–39 | 5.6 | 12.5 | 45 |
| 1945–49 | 4.1 | 9.0 | 46 |
| 1955–59 | 5.3 | 13.1 | 40 |
| 1965–69 | 3.4 | 14.2 | 24 |
| 1975–79 | 6.0 | 15.5 | 39 |
| 1984–85 | 4.1 | 19.7 | 21 |

SOURCES: U.S. Department of Agriculture, *Agricultural Statistics;* and *Cotton and Wool: Outlook and Situation Yearbook,* August 1985.

[3]In order to assure some immediate reduction in production, as the act was passed after the planting season, a plow-up program was instituted for cotton and tobacco. Farmers were paid to plow up a portion of these crops. A similar program was planned for wheat, but as a severe drought soon set in it became apparent that production would be down to desired levels without the crop destruction. A similar program was instituted in the livestock sector with the slaughter program for brood sows and pigs. Brood sows and young pigs were purchased by the government at premium prices and slaughtered in order to reduce pork production.

## World War II and Its Aftermath

Prior to World War II, agricultural price supports usually ranged from 52 to 75 percent of parity. During the war they were increased to 90 percent, allegedly to provide incentive for farmers to produce large crops. Wartime legislation promised high support levels (90 percent of parity) through 1948. There was little change in the high support policies until more flexible supports permitting lower prices were started under the Eisenhower administration in the 1950s (Appendix Table A-4).

Trends in the actual support levels are shown in Table 4.2. By 1950, supports for most crops had risen substantially faster than prices paid by farmers for all commodities, interest, taxes, and wage rates, indicating a great increase in incentive to produce (see Table 4.4). During the 10 years prior to the programs, 1922–23 to 1932–33, prices received by farmers declined an average of 6.5 percent per year, while the prices they paid declined at a slower 2.5 percent rate. In contrast, from 1932–33 to 1942–43, prices received by farmers rose at an average rate of 9.6 percent per year compared with an increase of 3.7 percent for items used in production. Furthermore, during the next 10 years, 1942–43 to 1952–53, farm product prices rose even faster, and farmers also received government payments averaging $205 million per year, or about 1.5 percent of net farm income (Appendix Table A-2). What's more, because of sharply increasing yields, incentives for increased production by farmers would have increased during this period even if the parity ratio had declined.

---

*Table 4.4*

RATES OF CHANGE, AVERAGE PRICE RECEIVED FOR
FARM PRODUCTS SOLD AND AVERAGE PRICE PAID
FOR ITEMS USED IN FARM PRODUCTION (%)

| Period | Price Received | Price Paid |
|---|---|---|
| 1922–23 to 1932–33 | −6.5 | −2.5 |
| 1932–33 to 1942–43 | 9.6 | 3.7 |
| 1942–43 to 1952–53 | 4.5 | 5.4 |

SOURCES: *Economic Report of the President*, 1986; and U.S. Department of Agriculture, *Agricultural Statistics*, 1946, 1956, and 1984.

## Other Countervailing Policies

As indicated in Table 4.5, the use of primary plant nutrients (nitrogen, phosphate, and potash), which had declined from 5.76 to 5.04 pounds per acre in the 10 years prior to the programs, more than doubled from 1932–33 to 1942–43. The use of liming materials increased twelvefold. The increase in per-acre use of the primary plant nutrients accelerated as price supports were sharply increased.

In addition to the guaranteed high prices, part of the incentive for the soil enrichment inputs was provided by government cost sharing for soil conservation practices. Payments were made to farmers after 1936 for applications of commercial fertilizer, liming, planting green manure and cover crops, terracing, contour farming, drainage, irrigation, pasture seeding, fire protection, and weed control. Payments usually amounted to about 50 percent of the estimated cost of such practices. They were often contingent upon shifting more acres into grasses and legumes, but they also provided incentive for using more fertilizer on crops grown under the acreage allotment programs. In 1952–53, payments totaled $266 million, equivalent to one-fourth of the total expenditures of U.S. farmers for fertilizer and lime. Because these measures improved the yields of crops, they tended to defeat the purpose of the acreage control programs.

Aid to farmers in the form of research and education was also expanded rapidly following the AAA programs. Expanded agricultural research was carried on at numerous state and federal stations around the country. The results were disseminated to farmers through state Agriculture Extension Services, with offices and trained personnel in practically every county of the nation. An entirely new agency, the Soil Conservation Service, was created to assist in soil enrichment.

As indicated in Table 4.6, the growth of these farm support agencies was rapid during the first phase of the farm programs. Outlays for both farm research and extension increased at a higher rate than the wholesale price index during the 20 years ending in 1952–53. By 1952, the Soil Conservation Service had 11,675 full-time employees, almost equal to the Extension Service field staff of 12,600. The efforts of these people, too, helped increase production.

Special cooperative credit agencies for supplying agricultural loans had been established with federal assistance prior to the New Deal.

*Table 4.5*

TREND IN USE OF PRIMARY PLANT NUTRIENTS

| Nutrient | Pounds per Harvested Acre | | | | Rate of Change (%) | | |
|---|---|---|---|---|---|---|---|
| | 1922–23 | 1932–33 | 1942–43 | 1952–53 | 1922–23 to 1932–33 | 1932–33 to 1942–43 | 1942–43 to 1952–53 |
| Nitrogen | 1.22 | 1.31 | 2.64 | 8.98 | 0.7 | 7.3 | 13.0 |
| Phosphate | 3.20 | 2.53 | 6.89 | 13.10 | −2.3 | 10.5 | 6.6 |
| Potash | 1.34 | 1.20 | 3.46 | 9.73 | −1.1 | 11.2 | 10.9 |
| Total | 5.76 | 5.04 | 13.00 | 31.82 | −1.3 | 9.9 | 9.4 |
| Liming materials | 20.29 | 9.71 | 114.33 | 140.53 | −7.1 | 28.0 | 2.1 |

SOURCE: U.S. Department of Agriculture, *Economic Indicators of the Farm Sector: Production and Efficiency Statistics*, 1981 and 1984.

*Table 4.6*

AVERAGE COST OF USDA PROGRAMS
AND WHOLESALE PRICE INDEX
($ MILLIONS)

| Source of Cost | 1932–33 | 1952–53 | % Change |
|---|---|---|---|
| Soil Conservation Service | 0.2 | 57.8 | 18,900 |
| Research | 19.4 | 55.0 | 184 |
| Extension Service | 10.0 | 32.6 | 226 |
| Wholesale price index (1967 = 100) | 33.81 | 88.0 | 160 |

SOURCES: Murray R. Benedict, *Can We Solve the Farm Problem?* (New York: Twentieth Century Fund, 1955), p. 556; and *Economic Report of the President.*

The Farm Loan Act of 1916 authorized 12 regional Federal Land Banks for supplying long-term farm real estate credit. In 1923, 12 Federal Intermediate Credit Banks were established for rediscounting non–real estate farm loans of commercial banks and other lenders so that such loans could be made for longer periods of time. Although some government assistance was provided in the form of initial capital, these agencies were designed to make loans without further government subsidies. Hence, they were largely self-supporting prior to the Great Depression.

In the late 1920s, the government began to make special disaster-type loans to farmers on a subsidized basis. At first they were made only during periods of extreme hardship, but by the 1930s they had become almost an annual occurrence. Beginning in 1933, sizable temporary subsidies were advanced to the Federal Land Banks for reducing their rates of interest on previously made loans to farmers (Benedict 1955, 150–51).

Government-subsidized farm credit took on characteristics of permanency in the mid-1930s with the creation of the Resettlement Administration. The Resettlement Administration was set up as an independent government agency for the resettlement of destitute or low-income families so that they could become self-supporting. It made subsidized loans based on an approved farm and home management plan supervised by representatives of the lending agency.

Loans outstanding to farmers under this program—transferred

to the Farm Security Administration (FSA) in 1937 and renamed the Farmers Home Administration (FmHA) in 1946—averaged about $500 million per year during the period 1946–49, or about 4 percent of total farm credit outstanding. Although such credit probably offset some commercial credit to farmers and did not indicate an equivalent addition to farm resources, it surely led to some increase in farm output. Hence, in addition to being wealth transfers from the rest of the economy to the recipients, such funds served to further assist in defeating the reduced farm output objectives of the acreage reduction programs.

**Summary**

From the beginning, the acreage withdrawal and other supply-control provisions put forward by the Agricultural Adjustment Administration were leaky. Farmers soon discovered a variety of methods to maximize their economic position while adhering to the letter of the law's requirements. When paid to withdraw land from tillage, they retired only their least fertile plots. They practiced more intensive cultivation on the land they kept in circulation. They switched from controlled crops such as corn to noncontrolled crops such as soybeans. For all these reasons, total farm output remained high despite all of the AAA's expensive efforts to reduce the supply of farm commodities.

Another problem was that the New Deal policies were at war with themselves. By sharply raising commodity price support levels during World War II and in the decades following, the government increased the individual farmer's incentive to produce. At the same time, the higher consumer prices reduced demand, both at home and abroad, and led to substitution (such as artificial fibers for cotton). The Smoot-Hawley and other tariffs of the early 1930s further damaged agricultural exports.

Other government programs also worked against the stated goal of reduced farm output and permanently increased farm prices. Federal research and farmer education were stepped up. Large subsidies for soil improvement were established, and farm credit subsidies took on permanent form in the mid-1930s.

Together, all of these supply-enhancing, price-increasing measures defeated government efforts to reduce agricultural overproduction.

# 5. The Second Phase: Surplus Problems and Export Subsidies

Following the huge buildup of farm commodity surpluses in the wake of high postwar price supports and failure of the production control programs, the Eisenhower administration in 1953 was faced with the necessity for a change. Unlike his predecessors, the incoming secretary of agriculture, Ezra Taft Benson, had received training in economics and recognized that high price supports were the core of the problem. Soon after taking office he wrote,

> The farmers' basic problems . . . are due in large part to Government price and acreage control policies. These took away the initiative of management, making it impossible for farmers to make the most efficient use of their machinery. Continued indefinitely, these policies would have driven free farmers to a condition of peasantry. The high, rigid price supports which have been maintained were never responsible for the high prices the farmer received during the war periods. Prices were higher than the supports and insofar as their effect on farm income was concerned the supports might just as well not have been on the statute books.
>
> But their continuation after the war has had a most harmful effect. Their principal result has been to pile up, in government bins, surpluses of farm products that have hung over the market like the sword of Damocles (Benson 1956, 27).

After serving almost eight years as secretary of agriculture he concluded that the same problem still existed: "The nub of our present problem is unrealistic support prices and futile attempts to control production" (Benson 1960, 23). Nevertheless, Benson had reservations about a return to free agricultural markets and maintained that some price supports for farm products were necessary:

> Price supports should provide insurance against disaster to the farm producing plant and help stabilize national food supplies. But, price supports which tend to prevent production shifts toward a balanced supply in terms of demand and which encourage

43

uneconomic production and result in continuing heavy surpluses and subsidies should be avoided (Benson 1962, 603).

Despite his skepticism about the existing farm program, Benson believed that agriculture was an economic special case and could not operate profitably within a free competitive system without government support. What was needed, the new administration believed, was merely a retreat from the excesses of the earlier program.

Under Eisenhower and Benson, the old framework of acreage controls and price supports was retained but liberalized, and some new programs were grafted on to achieve short-run economic viability. Less than a month after taking office, the administration removed all price and distribution controls from livestock and meat (U.S. Department of Agriculture 1980, Bulletin 425:72). The major crop programs, however, which were the heart of the problem, were treated much more gently. The acreage controls were made more restrictive through a soil bank program and cross-compliance checks among cooperating farmers. Support prices became less rigid, and new programs were instituted to increase exports of U.S. farm products. Efforts to increase world consumption of U.S. agricultural output through massive gifts and export subsidies were the most significant of the 1950s reforms.

**Production Controls Tightened**

The Agricultural Acts of 1954 and 1956 inched toward market pricing of farm products, using what Secretary Benson referred to as "price flexibility to help keep commodity supplies in balance with markets" (Benson 1962, 290). They also led to increased restrictions on total farm production. The chief tool toward that end was the Soil Bank, authorized in 1956. The Soil Bank had two objectives: first, to bring about an immediate "voluntary" cut in production of the crops then in greatest surplus; second, to pay farmers in a long-run program known as the Conservation Reserve to shift land out of cultivation and into forage, trees, ponds, reservoirs, and so forth. Heretofore, acreage controls had been limited to individual crops, but with the Soil Bank the entire cropland of a farm became involved in the withdrawal process. The idea was that the total capacity of the farming industry was too large and that government action was necessary to reduce it to levels compatible with political benchmarks for farm prices and incomes.

In addition to reducing total acres available for crop production, the Soil Bank program required tighter compliance with crop-specific acreage allotments. The attempt was to reduce the shift to secondary crops that was defeating the original land retirement payments. The Soil Bank extended government controls by limiting the *total* acreage of crops grown. It was the beginning of the cross-compliance provisions of later years, which further limited the farmers' freedom to choose alternative crops. Production decisions about acreage used for individual crops were increasingly made by the federal government.

## Flexible Price Supports

Although it increased controls in the area of production limits, the new administration recognized that price controls and supports were a primary cause of trouble and some surpluses. Unfortunately, the administration had little cooperation from Congress in remedying that problem. Soon after taking office Secretary Benson found that a majority of both houses opposed his proposals to lower price supports. Thus, a crucial debate on the nation's farm programs began.[1] Fortunately for the administration, two former Democratic agriculture secretaries, Clinton P. Anderson and, belatedly, Henry A. Wallace, realized the folly of high support prices and supported the new flexible price proposals.

Benson defended the administration's position that government supports should provide insurance against disaster to the farming industry and help stabilize national food supplies but should not be high enough to cause uneconomic production and heavy surpluses (Benson 1962, 602–5). Nevertheless, he continued to be vehemently opposed by most Democrats and a number of leading Republicans from farm communities.

Leaders of the opposition to flexible price supports relied less on economic arguments than on the view that other industries had an unfair advantage over agriculture under market conditions and that

[1]This excludes the more limited debate during the previous administration when the Brannan Plan conflicted with the high price support views of Congress. It was then proposed that the purchasing power of farmers be maintained (at high levels) by direct payments from the U.S. Treasury to farmers.

45

the plentiful supply and low cost of food American consumers enjoyed justified collective aid to farmers. They proposed to deplete government surpluses by increasing exports through subsidies and donations. John Kenneth Galbraith, professor of economics at Harvard University, expressed the view that improvements in agricultural policy could best be achieved by recognizing that government support for the bargaining power of farmers is normal, that those economic agents with whom farmers deal have market power ipso facto, while the farmer must be given market power (Galbraith 1955, 214–15).

With little sentiment within either the administration or Congress for entirely eliminating government intervention in the market for farm products, a compromise was reached in 1954. It called for the agriculture secretary to set price supports on basic crops that would result in "parity" ranging from 82.5 percent to 90 percent in 1955, and from 75 percent to 90 percent thereafter. In 1956, however, opponents managed to get a bill through Congress that called for a return to the 90 percent of parity support level. It was vetoed by the president. In 1958, President Eisenhower requested legislation to permit further lowering of price supports for basic commodities to 60 percent of parity, but Congress refused.

The extent of the move toward market pricing during this period is indicated by the CCC loan rates on some major commodities as shown in Table 5.1. Support prices for most major crops were

### Table 5.1
### CCC LOAN RATES ON MAJOR COMMODITIES

| Commodity | 1954 | 1958 | 1962 |
|---|---|---|---|
| Upland cotton (middling one inch) (¢ per lb.) | 34.0 | 35.1 | 32.5 |
| Corn (no. 3 yellow Chicago) ($ per bu.) | 1.58 | 1.18 | 1.17 |
| Grain sorghum (no. 2 yellow, Kansas City) ($ per bu.) | 1.34 | 1.06 | 1.14 |
| Peanuts (¢ per lb.) | 10.3 | 10.2 | 11.1 |
| Wheat (no. 2 hard winter, Kansas City) ($ per bu.) | 2.53 | 2.14 | 2.27 |

SOURCE: U.S. Department of Agriculture, Agricultural Stabilization and Conservation Service, *Commodity Credit Corporation Charts*, June 30, 1975.

reduced during the years 1954–62. Sizable reductions were made in supports for corn (26 percent), wheat (10 percent), and grain sorghum (15 percent). Supports were reduced somewhat for cotton.

Overall prices measured by the consumer price index rose 12.5 percent during this period, 8 percent by the wholesale price index. Consequently, even with a stable level of price supports the prices of farm products relative to other prices would have declined about 10 percent. In real terms, then, the reduction in farm prices was even greater. Nonetheless, CCC outlays for price supports remained very high in the early 1960s, indicating that support prices continued to be well above market levels and that farmers were provided continuing incentive to produce more commodities than would clear an untampered market.

**Actions to Increase Demand**

A cornerstone of the new approach to farm programs beginning in the mid-1950s was intensive merchandising of farm products and consumption subsidizing at home and abroad. A major legislative step in this direction was the Agricultural Trade Development and Assistance Act of 1954, otherwise known at P.L. 480 and later the Food for Peace Act. Its stated purpose was to encourage the export of price-supported commodities to nations unable to make commercial purchases and to aid agricultural improvement in the developing nations.

Domestic food subsidy programs were also expanded to make use of larger amounts of surplus farm products. In 1954 a special school lunch milk program was established. It was expanded in 1956 to include institutions such as nonprofit summer camps and orphanages. In 1959 legislation was approved authorizing the secretary of agriculture to carry out a food stamp program similar to that of 1939–43 whereby food could be distributed to low-income families on a subsidized basis. Also, direct distribution of surplus products to low-income families was increased.

*Public Law 480: Humanitarianism or Export Dumping?*

Most farm commodities sold on concessional terms under P.L. 480 were transactions under Title I government-to-government credit agreements. The governments of less developed countries entered into agreements with the government of the United States to purchase agricultural commodities in this country and to pay for them largely with inconvertible local currency. The foreign currencies acquired in payment for the exports were to be recycled back into the importing nations for development projects (U.S. Department of Agriculture 1976, Handbook 345:65).

In its early years, P.L. 480 was lauded. Secretary Benson wrote, "Some parts of the surplus disposal program proved amazingly successful. In February 1954 the CCC held peak stocks of 1,200,000,000 pounds of cottonseed oil. A year and a half later we had not only disposed of these stocks, we had moved out an additional 250,000,000 pounds acquired in the meantime" (Benson 1962, 255). Similar successes were alleged for dairy products and soybeans. Yet the reductions in those commodities were more than offset by fast-growing stocks of wheat, corn, and other crops. And there was a dilemma at the heart of the program, namely that as surpluses were reduced, price supports had to be raised. Support levels moved up to 90 percent of parity as the surpluses were nearly depleted, thereby providing incentive for greater output and rebuilding the surpluses.

By 1953, the value of U.S. farm exports had declined to 72 percent of the peak 1951 level. Western European and Japanese agriculture was recovering, U.S. exports were costly because of high price supports, and exports financed through Lend-Lease, United Nations relief, and Mutual Security were declining. With P.L. 480 assistance beginning in 1954, exports began to move sharply upward again. By 1956, they were above the 1951 level.

As shown in Table 5.2, annual exports rose from an average of $3.2 billion in 1949–53 (prior to P.L. 480) to an average of $3.8 billion during 1954–58, the first five years under the act. The total continued upward, to $5.1 billion in 1961, eventually peaking at $40.5 billion in 1980. Exports rose from 10.5 percent of gross farm income in 1949–53 to 12.1 percent in 1954–58 following the large P.L. 480 export subsidies and sales in foreign currencies.

How much the government assistance affected total export volume is difficult to measure. It surely reduced the market for commercial sales by both the United States and friendly exporting nations such as Canada, Argentina, and Australia. U.S. commercial sales declined from $1.9 billion per year during 1949–53 to $1.7 billion during 1954–58 (Table 5.2). But by the late 1950s commercial sales

## Table 5.2

COMMERCIAL AND GOVERNMENT-ASSISTED AGRICULTURAL
EXPORTS BEFORE AND AFTER P.L. 480
($ MILLIONS)

| | 1949–53 Average[1] | 1954–58 Average | 1959 | 1960 | 1961 | 1962 |
|---|---|---|---|---|---|---|
| P.L. 480 sales | — | 1,012 | 1,143 | 1,386 | 1,586 | 1,535 |
| Mutual Security (AID) | — | 327 | 167 | 186 | 74 | 14 |
| Commercial sales with government assistance | — | 800 | 1,300 | 1,300 | 1,100 | 700 |
| Total exports with government assistance | 1,319 | 2,139 | 2,610 | 2,872 | 2,760 | 2,249 |
| Exports without assistance | 1,922 | 1,700 | 1,900 | 2,100 | 2,400 | 2,900 |
| Total exports | 3,241 | 3,800 | 4,500 | 4,900 | 5,100 | 5,100 |
| Gross cash income | 30,822 | 31,359 | 34,556 | 34,957 | 36,898 | 38,472 |

SOURCES: U.S. Department of Agriculture, *Agricultural Statistics*, 1965, pp. 594, 601; *Economic Indicators of the Farm Sector: National Financial Summary*, 1985; and Murray R. Benedict, *Can We Solve the Farm Problem?* (New York: Twentieth Century Fund, 1955), p. 559 (for 1949–53 exports with government assistance).
[1]Sizable quantities were exported with government assistance during this period. Wheat subsidies were provided based on the International Wheat Agreement, and other products were exported under the Surplus Property Act of 1944, the Foreign Aid Act of 1947, the Foreign Assistance Act of 1948, and the Mutual Assistance Act of 1953.

were again on the upswing, and by 1960 they amounted to $2.1 billion, somewhat above the pre–P.L. 480 level.

Government-assisted exports of farm commodities predated enactment of P.L. 480. Small subsidies were provided as early as 1932. Large programs developed during World War II, costing $2.1 billion in 1944. Subsidies were reduced following peace, rose again during the Korean conflict, then declined. They stood at less than $0.5 billion in 1953.

In addition to P.L. 480's success or failure in reducing surpluses, one must consider its effect on economic development in the less developed nations and its impact on world trade.

*Effects of Food Shipments on Less Developed Economies*

Since the food-importing nations reimbursed the United States for only about 10 percent of the original CCC investment in food, about 90 percent of the P.L. 480 shipments were essentially a gift by the United States to the recipient nations. Unfortunately, those gifts exacerbated the long-run food production problems in many recipient nations. While consumers pay less for food as the supply increases, domestic farmers are subjected to further food price declines. The lower prices reduce food production, thereby leading to less domestic food output in future years. Hence, these gifts contribute to further rural poverty in the recipient nations.

The cost of the grain to the importing nations, although relatively small, has some impact on their balance-of-payments, thereby reducing their ability to purchase other goods and services from abroad.

The shipments provided additional net food resources to the recipient countries and made some contribution to their welfare in the short-run. In the longer run, however, such gifts have an unfavorable impact on the recipient nations. They affect producers in the United States and in the food recipient nations in opposite directions. Here, the government purchases cause an increase in the price of grain to producers and the price of food to consumers. U.S. farmers are provided incentive to further increase production. In contrast, the gift leads to lower prices for farmers in the recipient nations and reduces their incentive to produce. As a result, each country moves even further in the wrong direction, and the recipient nations become even more dependent on the donor nations (Luttrell 1982, 11–13).

*Impact on World Trade: The Turnaround from Monopolistic Pricing to Dumping*

The impact of P.L. 480 was opposite that of the first phase of the farm programs. The earlier acreage control and price support programs tended to raise the price and to reduce the quantity of U.S. farm products flowing into international markets. Consequently, U.S. farm policies were looked upon favorably by farmers in other nations, including Australia, New Zealand, Canada, and Argentina, which exported farm commodities in competition with U.S. exports. Farmers in areas that imported U.S. products, such as Western Europe, were also pleased with our programs because they established world commodity prices at artificially high levels, resulting in somewhat higher prices for their own farm products. (Of course, U.S. and world *consumers* were negatively affected by our artificially high food and fiber prices.)

The first phase of the farm programs, carried out in the 1930s and 1940s, had effects similar to those of OPEC in restricting supply and raising oil prices in the 1970s. For a quarter of a century we restricted shipments of farm products to the rest of the world just as the OPEC countries restricted petroleum exports, charging food- and fiber-importing nations artificially high prices (the support price level) for the products.

Then with P.L. 480, U.S. policies suddenly moved to the other extreme. Instead of acting as a cartel we began exporting farm products at greatly reduced subsidized prices, dumping them on world markets, thereby upsetting production patterns in other nations where farm production had increased in response to our earlier price support programs.[2] Friendly exporting nations such as Canada, Australia, and Argentina found this reversal of earlier price and free trade policies particularly disruptive.

*Program Costs Continue to Rise*

Despite the strenuous efforts of the Eisenhower administration to reduce governmental activity in the farm sector, the cost of farm programs continued to rise sharply. While much of the real costs were hidden in budgetary accounting practices, in overvaluing the commodities used for foreign aid, and in higher prices to consumers, the data indicate that farm program costs may have tripled from the early 1950s to the early 1960s.[3]

[2]Although P.L. 480 and other export subsidy programs were designed to avoid interference with commercial markets as much as possible, there is little doubt but that such interference was great since the products shipped under the programs are fungible, and in some cases the recipient governments charged their citizens for them as though they were commercial products.

[3]Part of the cost of farm programs, for example, may be included in Defense or State Department budgets where counterpart funds are used by these agencies for expenditures in the food recipient nations. Such expenditures were no doubt greater than they would have been had not the counterpart funds existed on the balance sheets.

Direct payments to farmers plus net CCC losses in inventory operations, export payments, and interest rose from $654 million in 1954 to $2.8 billion in 1962 near the peak of P.L. 480 operations (Appendix Table A-2). And these costs probably accounted for less than 50 percent of all government farm subsidy outlays. Other losses included costs of the P.L. 480 exports and expenses from the International Wheat Agreement, the National Wool Act, the transfer of bartered materials to a supplemental stockpile, cost sharing for soil conservation practices, crop insurance losses, and the portion of nutrition program costs attributable to the farm programs. USDA outlays for all purposes totaled $2.6 billion in 1954 and $6.7 billion in 1962 (Appendix Table A-1).

In fairness, part of the sharply rising losses beginning in the mid–1950s were the unavoidable result of large surplus accumulations from earlier years. But the net result was that Department of Agriculture outlays for all purposes rose from 4 percent of the federal budget in 1954 to 6 percent in 1962 (Appendix Table A-1).

### Summary

By the early 1950s the excessive costs relative to benefits of the New Deal farm programs were apparent to all, including the Eisenhower administration. Artificially high price supports for major crops had led to an enormous buildup of surpluses. Furthermore, farm production continued to grow despite the acreage controls in effect.

The program unfolded by the new administration involved more rigid production controls, a move toward lowering the incentive to produce through "flexible" (lower) support prices, and measures intended to increase demand for agricultural products. The cropland base was reduced somewhat through a Soil Bank program and by requiring cross-compliance among farmers participating in government land retirement schemes, so that shifts to secondary, non-controlled crops did not defeat the purposes of the controls. These new measures were somewhat effective in slowing increases in agricultural output, but they tightened the government's grip on farm production decisions in the process.

The move toward flexible price supports was a basic shift toward more effective solutions. It reduced the incentive of farmers to increase production of crops already in surplus stocks. Unfortunately, the price reductions were not sufficient to bring supply and demand into balance and the unwanted surpluses of most commodities continued, albeit at reduced levels.

On the demand side, the major program change was a massive government-subsidized export plan authorized under Public Law 480. This program allegedly sold surpluses to relieve hunger and support economic development in the less developed nations. Actually, the food was largely a gift, often retarding agricultural development and causing other problems in the recipient nations. The program was also counter to the liberal trade policies the United States advocated. Friendly competing exporters viewed the program as agricultural "dumping."

Meanwhile, the cost of the government farm programs continued to spiral, roughly tripling from the early 1950s to the early 1960s.

# 6. The Third Phase: Direct Payments

By the early 1960s, it was increasingly evident that national objectives for farm commodity prices and incomes could not be achieved with the tools then in use. While national income was rising steadily, net farm income had fallen below the levels of the early 1950s (Appendix Table A-1).

Mechanization and improved technology were bringing rapid increases in farm productivity. Agricultural output per manhour changed little from 1915 to 1935, doubled from 1935 to 1950, then more than doubled from 1950 to 1965. Labor requirements for farm production thus declined sharply, dropping 33 percent during the 1950s and another 38 percent during the 1960s. Agriculture was beset with excessive labor resources throughout most of this period, with lagging movement of workers from farm to nonfarm occupations. At the same time, excessive nonlabor resources moved into the industry as a result of incentives provided by the price support and income payments programs.

Direct government payments to farmers had been made on a small scale in the form of acreage rentals since the 1930s, largely for soil conservation purposes. In most years they amounted to no more than 2 percent of net farm operator income. As it became apparent, however, that the income goals of farmers and government policymakers could not be achieved with the price supports, acreage controls, and subsidies in effect during the 1950s, a gradual shift toward direct payments to producers commenced. With the establishment of the Soil Bank program in 1956, direct payments jumped, rising from an average of $263 million per year in 1950–54 to $714 million in 1955–59 (Appendix Table A-3). Direct checks from the U.S. government to farm producers were becoming a sizable factor in farm income and taxpayer expense.

The Soil Bank's acreage reserve program terminated in 1958 but was followed by an acreage diversion program for corn and other feed grains in the 1961 Agricultural Act, under which payments were made to producers directly. The Agricultural Act of 1965 continued the feed grain and cotton acreage diversion programs. The Agricultural Act of 1970 initiated an acreage set-aside program for wheat, feed grains, and cotton. Direct payments continued to escalate.

## Target Pricing

Cropland set-aside and diverted acreage payments were continued in the Agricultural and Consumer Protection Act of 1973, but at this time an entirely new system of direct payments—target pricing—was devised for making direct payments to farmers. Under this system direct payments were made to producers to bridge the gap between the market price and the support price set by the government (U.S. Department of Agriculture 1976, Agricultural Handbook 345:16–18).[1]

Target pricing thus freed policymaking from the dilemma of accumulating commodity surpluses and then having to adjust farm prices in order to slow or reduce those accumulations. It permitted administrators greater flexibility. Farm incomes would be maintained at desired levels by increasing or decreasing the direct payments to farmers, not by manipulating markets.

Because transfer payments rather than price fixings were the

---

[1]While the level of the support price (target price) was still politically determined, the Food and Agricultural Act of 1977 authorized a support price for feed grains for the years 1979–81 at the 1978 level adjusted for changes in the cost of production. This was not the first attempt to tie farm price supports to production costs. The original parity concept in the 1933 Agricultural Adjustment Act was itself an attempt to relate farm commodity prices to production costs, and the 1949 amendments added some production costs to the parity index.

The argument for supporting farm prices at cost of production, however, contains all the handicaps of all other price support schemes. First, there are several different concepts of cost of production, that is, marginal cost and average costs. Second, there are more than two million farms in the nation, each with a different marginal and average cost. Hence, any likely level of price support selected for a farm commodity will be above the cost of production for some and below the cost for all others.

Consequently, any price support level that may be authorized by law contains all the handicaps of all other price support schemes. If the support price is above the market price for the commodity, it will provide incentives for increased output and result in a "surplus" of the commodity. If it is below the market price, it will be ineffective and useless (for a more extensive discussion of this topic, see Luttrell 1977).

instruments of the new policy, food costs to domestic consumers were lowered, and U.S. farm products became more competitive in world markets. The use of direct export subsidies, which were strenuously opposed by our allies during the period of massive P.L. 480 shipments, could now be reduced without much loss to farmers. Although U.S. farm products were still subsidized, the new system created less international friction. Subsidies involved in producer payments were less obvious.

## Direct Payments Reveal Costs and Benefits

While target pricing and direct payments covering the difference between the market price and the desired price achieved the objective of raising farm incomes, the system was not free of shortcomings. For one, direct payments under the new regimen rose from nil in 1960 to almost $3 billion, or 30 percent of net farm income, in 1970. Heretofore, much of the cost of programs designed to enhance farm incomes was concealed in payments for such publicly appealing functions as soil conservation, Food for Peace, better diets for the poor, economic development of less developed nations, and similar activities. But the beneficiaries and amounts of direct payments were more difficult to hide. And as program costs continued to mount in the 1980s, taxpayer and budget concerns grew large.

Arguments for U.S. farm programs traditionally stressed aggregate farm income enhancement, with little attention paid to distribution of the benefits among the 2.3 million individual farmers. Now with open disparities in benefits ranging from a hundred dollars or less for one person to a million dollars or more for another, interest grew in finetuning the payments. Indicative of this concern was the limit established in 1974 of $20,000 to any one person. It did not apply, however, to CCC purchases and loans, and it was later raised to $50,000.

The increase was essential to induce larger farmers to comply with acreage restrictions. When their potential benefits from the program were capped at relatively low levels, they lost all incentive not to plant. That increased production and widened the gap between market and support prices. Even payments at the $50,000 limit were insufficient to induce many of the nation's largest farmers to comply with average restrictions. But direct checks of $50,000 from taxpayers to the more wealthy farmers caused a political problem.

By 1985, direct payments to farmers, excluding payments-in-kind, accounted for 23 percent of net farm income. This was down sharply from 37 percent in 1983 but above the level of 20 percent in 1970.

In the early 1970s, reduced trade barriers, large Russian grain purchases, and other factors led to a sharp increase in agricultural exports. Production controls could be relaxed somewhat and most surpluses were liquidated. (Exports represented one-fourth of all farm commodity sales in 1975, versus just 15 percent in 1970.) As a result, farm commodity prices and incomes rose sharply. From 1970 to 1973 the index of farm prices climbed 59 percent. Net farm income to operators more than doubled, from $14.4 billion to $34.4 billion (Appendix Table A-1). Income remained relatively high through 1975. Market factors brought another spurt in prices and farm incomes in 1978 and 1979. Gradually, however, agricultural prices and incomes moved back down in the late 1970s, and by the early 1980s, farm program costs were again on the upswing.

Excessive incentive to produce was maintained through support prices based on the target price system and the loan rate, and by the early 1980s, surpluses held by the CCC grew large again (Appendix Table A-4). At the close of 1982, the value of all commodities owned by the CCC totaled $5.5 billion, up from $3.8 billion a year earlier, and loans outstanding on pledged commodities totaled $17.9 billion, up from $7.8 billion.

### Payment-in-Kind Emerges

With farm commodity surpluses bulging, and no change contemplated in the policies that caused the excess production, another variant to the numerous already complicated programs for transferring income from the nonfarm to the farm sector emerged.

Instead of writing checks to farmers who reduced crop acreage, the so-called Payment-in-Kind (PIK) scheme authorized the Department of Agriculture to give farmers surplus commodities held in storage by the CCC. Farmers could use the grain as feed or sell it at the prevailing market price. The impact of the program on market prices for grain was the same as if the government had sold all the grain at market prices (dumping it on the domestic market) and then transferred the proceeds to farmers. The alleged merit of PIK was that it emptied the grain bins at reduced government cost.

But the biggest advantage to government officials of structuring farm subsidy programs in forms such as PIK or loans on commodities at above market values or export subsidies or import quotas and marketing orders is that they are much easier to conceal than direct payments to individual farmers. Their problem, of course, is that indirect supports provide gains to the industry as a whole, on the basis of quantity marketed rather than welfare criteria. Not all farmers are poverty-stricken, but indirect programs are very hard to aim. By giving farmers commodities rather than checks, the government obscured the fact that moderate-income taxpayers were being taxed to enhance the incomes of many high-income farmers.

While the Agricultural Act of 1985 was hailed as a move to reduce farm program costs, there are no indications to date of cost reductions. It continues payment-in-kind awards to those farmers who comply with the acreage restrictions. For this reason, the market price for most crops will likely remain below the CCC support price, causing high program costs. Continued overproduction plus the government-induced revival of export subsidies in the form of market certificates will serve to keep world commodity prices low and to annoy friendly nations.

The market-certificate export subsidy under the 1985 Agricultural Act was limited to cotton and rice. It covers the difference between the CCC support price and the world price at the time of sale. Rice and cotton can thus be dumped on world markets in unlimited amounts so long as U.S. taxpayers are willing to foot the bill.

## Summary

Despite the massive export subsidy programs, acreage controls, and price support programs of the late 1950s, farm income lagged well behind nonfarm income in the 1960s, even though CCC losses on price support programs were mushrooming. Resentment of the P.L. 480 export subsidy program was also growing at home and abroad.

With this view of the farm picture, and feeling great pressure for additional aid, policymakers in the 1960s took a major step toward placing the farm sector of the nation's economy directly on the federal payroll. Direct government payments to farmers began to account for a sizable percentage of net farm income. As a vehicle for determining the amount of direct payments, target pricing was

# 7. Food Stamps and Farmers

"Feeding the hungry" has been a primary means of disposing of agricultural surpluses and increasing farm incomes since the farm programs began in the early 1930s. Helping Americans who are viewed as going to bed hungry evokes sympathy from a wide sector of public opinion and broadens political support for farm programs. The aims and interests of the "hunger lobby" have thus coalesced with those of farm subsidy supporters.[1]

Federally subsidized domestic food distribution programs began on a small scale in 1932 with wheat donations by the Federal Farm Board to the Red Cross. They continued at a moderate level during the 1930s through the Federal Surplus Relief Corporation, set up in 1933, and the Federal Surplus Commodities Corporation, set up in 1935. These programs were enlarged following World War II but remained a relatively small portion of the federal budget until the Food Stamp Act of 1964 greatly expanded the program. During the 1970s, subsidized food distributions, especially the food stamp program, accelerated sharply. They have become a major factor in the federal budget. The cost of the food stamp program alone exceeds $11 billion per year, or more than one-third of annual net farm income.

## Objective: Humanitarianism or Producer Gains?

Food and nutrition programs contain both humanitarian and farm price support features. But despite the rhetoric of moral responsibility for feeding the hungry, the dominant objective of the proponents of these programs during most of their existence has been higher returns to farmers. Evidence of this can be seen in the sources

[1]As reported by the U.S. Department of Treasury (1985, 17–18), the marriage of the two groups initially occurred during a vote to table an expanded food stamp bill. Northern Democrats on the House Rules Committee made it known that they were holding up a tobacco research bill (supported by producers) pending favorable action on a food stamp bill. Numerous deals linking the two groups occurred in later years.

of the programs' support, the specific commodities included in the gifts, and the fact that the distributions have been made through the Department of Agriculture, an agency designed primarily to aid farmers, rather than through other agencies.

In 1932, the chairman of the Federal Farm Board proposed the donation of 45 million bushels of wheat, about 50 percent of the board's holdings, to the American Red Cross for relief purposes. However, Sen. Reed Smoot (R–Utah) of Smoot-Hawley tariff fame, an advocate of producer interests, proposed and achieved the donation of the entire stock held by the board. He stated, "I think it would be better for the government, the farmer, and everybody else—even better for the whole country—if the whole thing were absolutely closed out. . . . This is hanging over the wheat market . . . like a pall" (Hadwiger 1970, 335).

Following the launch of the New Deal in 1933, humanitarian interest in distributions of surplus food stocks was represented by a Consumer Advisory Board in the National Recovery Administrations and the Consumers Council in the Agricultural Adjustment Administration. Consumer interests, however, were generally overruled by the more powerful producer interests since these agencies were dominated by individuals primarily responsible for furthering the interests of farmers and handlers (Benedict 1953, 337). In recognition of the dominant producer interest, the Federal Surplus Relief Corporation (FSRC) was placed in the Department of Agriculture in 1935. By this time it had become apparent that the FSRC was primarily an organization to assist the department in its surplus removal programs rather than an organization for relief of the indigent (Hadwiger 1970, 362).

In 1939 a food stamp plan was started for moving surplus foodstuffs into consumption. Under this plan families on relief were permitted to purchase food stamps for cash at a fraction of their face value. The stamps could be used to purchase selected foods in grocery stores. This subsidy increased the food buying power of low-income families and provided a wider range of subsidized products than the surplus distribution programs. It was only available, however, in limited areas. In addition, the program was open to only a small percentage of the population until the late 1960s (Table 7.1). Program coverage was greatly expanded under the Food Stamp Act of 1964 and again under the amendments of 1971 and

1973. Under these acts food stamps were placed under uniform national standards. Thereafter, food stamps gradually replaced most direct donations of surplus farm commodities to needy families. The program by then covered all U.S. counties, cities, and possessions, and the list of eligible foods that could be purchased had been broadened.

Other food assistance programs closely tied into farm surplus removal were inaugurated and expanded with the arrival of the high farm price support programs. Among the leading ones was the national school lunch program authorized in 1946, expanded in 1962, and expanded again in 1973. This program for providing free or reduced cost lunches to most school children operates in all 50 states and in most outlying possessions.

The use of food stamps rather than direct distributions of surplus farm commodities to the indigent greatly increased urban support for the programs. As the report *The Food Stamp Program: History, Description, Issues and Options*, prepared by the staff of the Senate Committee on Agriculture, Nutrition, and Forestry, concludes: "The impact of the Food Stamp Program in lowering commodity surpluses has been one of [its] cornerstones. . . . The Food Stamp Program has been used in legislative strategy to entice urban legislators who might not otherwise support costly farm price support programs to do so in exchange for rural support for the Food Stamp Program" (U.S. Senate Committee on Agriculture 1985, 325–27).

## The Takeoff in the 1970s

The food stamp program remained relatively insecure until the late 1960s, with only sporadic support in Congress and relatively small appropriations. In 1968 House and Senate conferees agreed to extend the food stamp program until December 31, 1970, to expire simultaneously with the farm bill. Authorization ceilings were set at $315 million for fiscal 1969, $340 million for 1970, and $170 million for the first half of 1971. Congress, however, appropriated only $280 million for the 1969 program. Reports of hunger and malnutrition during this period were frequent. *Hunger USA*, a report by the Citizens Board of Inquiry, was highly critical of all government food aid programs. It reported that 10 million to 14.5 million Americans were seriously underfed (U.S. Senate Committee on Agricul-

## Table 7.1
### COST OF AND PARTICIPATION IN FOOD STAMP AND COMMODITY DISTRIBUTION PROGRAMS

| Year | Cost[1] ($ Millions) | | Participation (Thousands of Participants) | | |
|---|---|---|---|---|---|
| | Food Stamps | Total Benefits[2] | Food Stamps | Total | % of Population |
| 1962 | 13 | 240 | 141 | 6,552 | 3.5 |
| 1963 | 19 | 223 | 358 | 5,908 | 3.1 |
| 1964 | 29 | 226 | 360 | 5,566 | 2.9 |
| 1965 | 33 | 259 | 633 | 5,375 | 2.8 |
| 1966 | 65 | 199 | 1,218 | 5,097 | 2.6 |
| 1967 | 106 | 207 | 1,832 | 4,836 | 2.5 |
| 1968 | 173 | 297 | 2,420 | 5,634 | 2.8 |
| 1969 | 229 | 454 | 3,222 | 6,761 | 3.4 |
| 1970 | 550 | 839 | 6,457 | 10,434 | 5.1 |
| 1971 | 1,523 | 1,845 | 10,549 | 14,191 | 6.9 |
| 1972 | 1,797 | 2,109 | 11,594 | 14,596 | 7.0 |
| 1973 | 2,131 | 2,386 | 12,107 | 14,548 | 6.9 |

## Table 7.1 (continued)

| Year | Cost[1] ($ Millions) | | Participation (Thousands of Participants) | | |
|---|---|---|---|---|---|
| | Food Stamps | Total Benefits[2] | Food Stamps | Total | % of Population |
| 1974 | 2,718 | 2,923 | 13,524 | 14,930 | 7.1 |
| 1975 | 4,386 | 4,442 | 19,238 | 19,326 | 8.9 |
| 1976 | 5,327 | 5,345 | 17,971 | 18,050 | 8.3 |
| 1977 | 5,067 | 5,078 | 16,097 | 16,181 | 7.4 |
| 1978 | 5,139 | 5,151 | 15,270 | 15,346 | 6.9 |
| 1979 | 6,480 | 6,512 | 19,296 | 19,401 | 8.7 |
| 1980 | 8,685 | 8,720 | 21,992 | 22,083 | 9.8 |
| 1981 | 10,630 | 10,724 | 22,431 | 22,519 | 9.7 |
| 1982 | 10,409 | 10,231 | 21,717 | 21,810 | 9.1 |
| 1983 | 11,152 | 11,178 | 21,625 | 21,732 | 9.2 |
| 1984 | 10,696 | 11,818 | 20,854 | — | — |
| 1985 | 10,744 | 11,828 | 19,902 | — | — |

SOURCES: U.S. Senate Committee on Agriculture, Nutrition, and Forestry, *The Food Stamp Program: History, Description, Issues and Options*, April 1985, p. 162; and U.S. Department of Agriculture, *Agricultural Statistics*, 1986 and 1987.

[1]Value of coupons issued less payments by participants.

[2]Excludes child nutrition, special supplemental food, and temporary emergency food assistance programs.

65

ture 1985, 31).[2] The Poor People's Campaign in 1968 urged free food stamps for the lowest income groups and the lowering of food stamp prices generally.[3]

In response to these demands, President Richard M. Nixon sent a request to Congress in May 1969 asking for an increase of $270 million for the food stamp program for fiscal 1970 and a $1 billion increase for the following year. Eligibility for food stamps was greatly liberalized. Many families could thereafter receive stamps free, and most low-income families were required to spend no more than 30 percent of their income on food. The bill submitted to Congress in June further required that all counties in the nation participate in the federal food programs (U.S. Senate Committee on Agriculture 1985, 32–33). This legislation marked the advent of a new cycle of massive government farm programs. The cost of food stamp distributions totaled only $65 million in 1966 and $106 million in 1967 (Table 7.1). By 1970, these outlays had jumped to $550 million, and they continued to increase at a high rate, reaching $10 billion by the early 1980s.

With farm producer interests combined with large urban interests by the food stamp program, legislating against hunger became a favorite activity in Congress. The major questions to be resolved at this stage concerned how much, if anything, the recipients of food stamps should pay, how to determine eligibility, and how large an appropriation would be required for the program. In 1970 the Food Stamp Act was amended, resulting in uniform and higher allotment schedules and larger benefits. Eligibility standards were thereafter determined by the federal government and they were usually more liberal than those of the states. Provision was made for incapacitated elderly recipients who used food stamps to purchase home-delivered meals.

The 1973 farm bill included a number of amendments to the Food Stamp Act. Items that could be purchased with food stamps were expanded to include seeds and garden plants, all imported foods, meals prepared for the elderly in certain communal dining rooms,

[2]A board formed at the request of Walter Reuther, head of the United Automobile Workers union.

[3]This was a group of low-income people gathered in Washington, D.C., to pressure Congress to expand various types of aid for the poor. They set up a "Resurrection City" of campsites on the Mall where thousands of people lived for several days.

meals prepared for narcotics addicts and alcoholics by their treatment programs, and hunting and fishing equipment for eligible households in remote areas of Alaska (U.S. Senate Committee on Agriculture 1985, 51). The appropriation for the program was again increased. Program-expanding bills and resolutions continued to proliferate, exceeding 15 for the year.

Although no major changes were made in the act in 1974, it was liberalized to some extent through disaster relief amendments. Appropriations were increased, and new measures were introduced in the House and Senate to provide food stamps on Indian reservations, to implement cost of living increases, to prohibit the use of food stamps to purchase imported meats, and to replace food stamps with cash assistance.

In 1975, the Ford administration attempted to brake the meteoric rise in food stamp expenditures by proposing that most food stamp recipients pay 30 percent of their net monthly income for food stamps. It was defeated in both houses by overwhelming majorities. Eligibility requirements were further liberalized during the year, and a supplemental appropriation was passed, bringing the total appropriation for the year to $4.8 billion. Legislative activity continued at a frenzied level with more than 120 food stamp–related bills introduced in Congress.

By 1977 it was increasingly recognized that the food stamp program was out of control. The Carter administration proposed and Congress enacted a complete revision of the program. The new act, effective in 1979, was expected to reduce benefits for about one-fourth of the existing recipients, to hold constant the benefits for one-half, and to increase benefits for one-fourth. The act attempted to place dollar limits on food stamp program costs, but both participation and costs continued to rise. New food stamp bills entered the legislative hopper at a high rate through the early 1980s, and the number of participants rose until 1980, by which time almost 10 percent of the population were beneficiaries of the program (Table 7.1).

Food stamp recipiency rose from 3.2 million persons in 1969 to 11.6 million in 1972, 18 million in 1976, and 22 million in 1980 (Table 7.1). Costs of the program rose even faster. From $65 million per year in 1966, expenditures rose to $550 million in 1970 and $8.7 billion in 1980, when the rate of increase slowed. Relative to net farm income, program expenses rose over the period 1966 to 1980 from less than 1 percent to 43 percent.

### Little Farm Income Gain

While the precise impact of the food stamp program on demand for farm products and on farm incomes is difficult to assess, it has certainly increased demand for farm products somewhat. On the basis of one economist's calculations of food spending patterns, the additional food purchased by lower-income Americans in 1985 as a result of food stamp availability totaled about $2.2 billion (Gardner 1981, 19). The farm value of such expenditures, however, accounted for only about 25 percent of the retail food costs or about $0.55 billion of the additional food expenditures. This is less than 0.5 percent of cash farm receipts estimated for 1986, so it is a small factor in farm income.[4] This is about the same impact as reported by the staff of the Senate Committee on Agriculture, which estimated that new food purchases as a result of the program amounted to less than 1.16 percent of the farm economy (U.S. Senate Committee on Agriculture 1985, 327).[5] It can therefore be seen that the food stamp program is not an important contributor to farm income.

### Summary

The food stamp program has grown from a small program in the 1930s to an $11 billion transfer scheme serving one American in ten during the 1980s. The period of fastest growth was from 1968 to 1978. The program has received broad political support in Congress because of its two-pronged objective: to increase farm incomes and alleviate hunger among the indigent. The farm sector supports it in order to achieve the first objective and urban interests support it to achieve the second.

However, the program is a failure in achieving the farm income objective. The increased spending on food resulting from the program probably accounts for less than 1 percent of total farm commodity sales.

[4]Gardner concluded that demand for food is increased by an income transfer only to the extent that spending on food is higher among recipients of the stamps than among the taxpayers who provided the funds.

[5]On the basis of this study, the $11 billion spent by the government on food stamps contributed $1.9 billion to the $166.6 billion gross farm income in 1985.

# 8. Subsidized Credit: Worsening Farm Poverty and Farm Debt Problems

Federally subsidized farm credit programs grew out of producer pressures for "more adequate" financing for agriculture. Assumed shortages of loan funds to meet the capital needs of plantation owners date back to colonial times and were important features of legislation involving public land disposal programs, banking, and farm cooperatives during the 1800s (Taylor 1952, 899–975). With rising farm commodity prices and land values in the early 1900s following depletion of the more productive public lands in the West, demands for government assistance in providing more adequate farm credit supplies rose. The alleged need for government subsidized credit was based on the argument that private lenders would not supply credit on repayment terms and in amounts required by farmers.

These pressures led the national conventions of both major political parties in 1912 to adopt resolutions in favor of rural credit assistance. Consequently, President Woodrow Wilson and Congress produced the Federal Farm Loan Act in 1916. It authorized the organization of the Federal Land Banks (FLBs) for making long-term farm mortgage loans. The banks were originally owned by the federal government, which purchased essentially all of the original capital stock. Later the Federal Intermediate Credit Banks (FICBs) and the Banks for Cooperatives (BCs) were authorized, and largely capitalized by the federal government, to supply credit for non–real estate and non–farm cooperative purposes. These three banking organizations, each composed of 12 regional banks, were organized into the Farm Credit System (FCS) in the early 1930s with a supervisory head, the Farm Credit Administration (FCA). The FLBs operate locally through Federal Land Bank Associations (FLBAs) and the FICBs through Production Credit Associations (PCAs) (Benedict 1955, 124–173).

Following capitalization by the government the FCS agencies

were designed to operate largely on their own with the usual cooperative privileges; that is, relief from some taxes on profits incurred by corporations. In addition, the FCS cooperatives are exempt from all federal, state, and local taxes except those on real estate, and holders of their debt instruments are exempt from all taxes except federal income taxes. Funds for lending are obtained largely through sales of notes, bonds, and debentures and borrowings from other financial institutions. Farmer borrowers are required to own stock, which further augments lending funds. Interest rates on loans to farmers are generally set at levels sufficient to cover costs and to provide for growing capital requirements. Security and collateral requirements have usually been about as strict as those of other private financial agencies. As a result of these relatively conservative operating practices the Farm Credit Banks had retired the original government capital by the late 1960s and, excluding the greater government supervision, were operating similarly to private credit agencies. But their allegedly conservative lending practices failed to pacify many farm groups, who contended that these agencies offered little in the way of farm credit that was not obtainable elsewhere. Hence, political agitation for lower-cost credit on more favorable terms to farmers continued (Benedict 1955, 124–73).

### Direct Government Credit to Farmers Emerges

In response to pressures by farm groups for more liberal credit, the government began prior to the Great Depression to make small-scale special or disaster-type loans to farmers at subsidized rates. These loans, first made under authority granted by the War Finance Corporation in 1918, were originally designed to direct capital to industries essential to the war effort rather than for farmer assistance. Following that, the Agricultural Credit Act of 1921 authorized loans to farmers indirectly through rural banks and farm cooperatives for feed, seed, and similar emergency relief purposes. The loans were available only to borrowers who were unable to obtain credit from private agencies. In succeeding years, disaster loans were authorized with increasing frequency, although generally limited to areas suffering from extreme hardship. By the late 1920s, they had become an annual occurrence. They remained of relatively small volume, under $6 million per year, or less than 1 percent of total farm debt, until farm commodity prices plunged at the onset of the Great Depression. In 1931, following the sharp downturn in farm income, authority for disaster loans was liberalized and the amount outstanding rose to $58 million, a tenfold increase in one year, and continued up in succeeding years.

In the mid-thirties, government-subsidized farm credit took on characteristics of permanency with creation of the Resettlement Administration. The Resettlement Administration was set up as an independent government agency for the resettlement of destitute or low-income families so that they could become self-supporting. It made subsidized loans, based on an approved farm and home management plan supervised by representatives of the lending agency (U.S. Department of Agriculture 1984, 2–3). This activity was transferred to the Department of Agriculture in 1937 and renamed the Farm Security Administration (FSA). As such it was the New Deal's answer to the national problem of hardship among tenant farmers.

In 1946, the FSA was restructured with passage of the Farmers Home Administration Act, eliminating some of the resettlement programs and incorporating others—including much of the emergency crop and feed loan programs—into the FmHA. Its early lending activities focused particularly on farm ownership, operations, and water projects in 17 western states. Amounts outstanding during the early years of the program, however, remained relatively small, totaling less than 5 percent of all farm real estate debt and only 0.3 percent of non–real estate debt in 1950 (Tables 8.1 and 8.2).

The amount of FmHA lending began to expand at a faster rate in 1949 when it was given authority to make rural housing and special emergency loans for the recovery of losses caused by natural disasters.

Amendments to the 1954 Water Facilities Act made government-subsidized credit available in rural areas for almost any conceivable purpose (U.S. Department of Agriculture 1984, 2–9).[1] For example, an amendment in 1961 made nonfarm rural residents eligible for FmHA loans. In 1962, a Senior Citizens Housing Act authorized

[1]By 1949, most farm emergency-type loans and standby arrangements for such credit had been transferred to the Farmers Home Administration from the Farm Credit Administration. Thereafter, emergency loans could be made promptly for such purposes as relief from local disasters, floods, droughts, and so forth. The FmHA had thus, in addition to aiding tenants and others to become landowners, become a lender of last resort to established farmers (Benedict 1955, 299–301).

71

*Table 8.1*

FARM REAL ESTATE DEBT BY REPORTING LENDER[1]
($ BILLIONS)

| Year | Federal Land Banks | Farmers Home Administration | Life Insurance Companies | Commercial Banks | Individuals and Others | Total | FmHA as % of Total |
|---|---|---|---|---|---|---|---|
| 1930 | 1.2 | — | 2.1 | 1.0 | 5.3[2] | 9.6 | — |
| 1935 | 1.9 | — | 1.3 | 0.5 | 3.9[2] | 7.6 | — |
| 1940 | 2.7 | 0.1 | 1.0 | 0.5 | 2.1 | 6.5 | 1.0 |
| 1945 | 1.3 | 0.2 | 0.9 | 0.5 | 1.9 | 4.8 | 3.9 |
| 1950 | 1.0 | 0.3 | 1.4 | 1.0 | 2.5 | 6.1 | 4.2 |
| 1955 | 1.5 | 0.4 | 2.3 | 1.3 | 3.6 | 9.0 | 4.6 |
| 1960 | 2.5 | 0.7 | 3.0 | 1.6 | 4.9 | 12.8 | 5.6 |
| 1965 | 4.2 | 1.5 | 4.8 | 2.6 | 8.0 | 21.2 | 7.1 |
| 1970 | 7.1 | 2.4 | 5.6 | 3.8 | 11.4 | 30.3 | 8.0 |
| 1975 | 16.0 | 3.4 | 6.7 | 6.3 | 17.3 | 49.7 | 6.8 |
| 1980 | 36.2 | 7.7 | 12.9 | 8.6 | 30.2 | 95.6 | 8.1 |
| 1985 | 44.6 | 10.4 | 11.8 | 11.4 | 27.2 | 105.4 | 9.9 |
| 1986 | 39.3 | 10.3 | 11.0 | 12.7 | 24.0 | 97.3 | 10.6 |

SOURCES: U.S. Department of Agriculture, *Economic Indicators of the Farm Sector: National Financial Summary,* 1985; and *Agricultural Statistics.*

[1]Includes operator households; excludes CCC price support loans.
[2]Includes joint stock banks and Federal Farm Mortgage Corporation.

*Table 8.2*

## NON-REAL ESTATE DEBT
### ($ BILLIONS)

| Year | Commercial Banks | Production Credit Association | Federal Intermediate Credit Banks | Farmers Home Administration | Individuals and Others | Total | FmHA as % of Total |
|---|---|---|---|---|---|---|---|
| 1930 | 2.5 | — | — | — | — | — | — |
| 1935 | 0.6 | 0.1 | 0.1 | 0.2 | — | — | — |
| 1940 | 1.0 | 0.2 | 0 | 0.5 | 1.7 | 3.3 | 13.8 |
| 1945 | 1.0 | 0.2 | 0 | 0.4 | 1.2 | 2.9 | 14.4 |
| 1950 | 2.5 | 0.5 | 0.1 | 0.3 | 2.8 | 6.1 | 5.4 |
| 1955 | 3.3 | 0.6 | 0.1 | 0.4 | 3.5 | 7.9 | 5.1 |
| 1960 | 5.0 | 1.5 | 0.1 | 0.4 | 5.0 | 12.0 | 3.1 |
| 1965 | 7.7 | 2.6 | 0.1 | 0.7 | 7.0 | 18.1 | 4.0 |
| 1970 | 11.1 | 5.3 | 0.2 | 0.8 | 4.8 | 22.3 | 3.6 |
| 1975 | 20.2 | 10.8 | 0.4 | 1.8 | 8.5 | 41.6 | 4.3 |
| 1980 | 31.6 | 19.7 | 0.8 | 11.8 | 17.7 | 81.6 | 14.4 |
| 1985 | 35.5 | 14.0 | 0.5 | 17.1 | 15.4 | 82.2 | 20.8 |
| 1986 | 31.2 | 11.3 | 0.3 | 16.4 | 12.4 | 71.6 | 22.9 |

SOURCES: U.S. Department of Agriculture, *Economic Indicators of the Farm Sector: National Financial Summary*, 1985; and *Agricultural Statistics*.

[1]Includes operator households; excludes CCC price support loans.
[2]Includes joint stock banks and Federal Farm Mortgage Corporation.

FmHA loans for low-rent apartment projects in rural communities. Amendments at this time also authorized loans to "family farmers" to set up farm-based recreational and other nonagricultural enterprises that would add to family income and authorized a pilot program for "rural renewal" and loans covering costs of other projects such as small watersheds in areas supervised by the USDA's Soil Conservation Service (U.S. Department of Agriculture 1984, 5).

The Economic Opportunity Act of 1964 further expanded FmHA lending authority to low-income rural people for small farm improvements and nonfarm enterprises that would add to family income. In 1966, senior citizens and younger low-income families became eligible for rural housing loans. Rural housing loans were further liberalized in the Housing Act of 1968, which permitted loans to low-income families at interest rates as low as 1 percent. In addition, subsidized loans were authorized to developers of low-priced rental housing and rural homesite development. Grants and loans of up to 90 percent of building costs were authorized for farm labor housing. The Housing Act of 1970 authorized the FmHA to cooperate with other farm mortgage lenders, taking a second mortgage where required, and in 1971 its farm ownership loan limit was raised from $60,000 to $100,000 (U.S. Department of Agriculture 1984, 5–6).

The Rural Development Act of 1972 further liberalized credit for farming and rural programs, including the guaranteeing of loans made by commercial lenders for farming, housing, and rural business. This program to encourage business and industrial development in rural areas (communities under 50,000 population) is primarily a guaranteed loan program whereby the FmHA guarantees the repayment of loans made by private lenders. The act raised the loan limit for loans on waste disposal systems and authorized loans for community halls, hospitals, nursing homes, and public recreation facilities. It also expanded the emergency loan program to farmers.

In 1974, a special Emergency Livestock Credit Act was passed authorizing FmHA to guarantee to commercial lenders loans made to livestock and poultry producers in financial distress. It permitted guarantees of commercial loans to eligible borrowers of up to $350,000. The 1978 Agricultural Credit Act authorized FmHA to make or guarantee loans of up to $400,000 to farmers or ranchers hard-pressed by "shortages" of credit from regular sources or by a cost-price squeeze (U.S. Department of Agriculture 1984, 7–8). It also authorized farm loans to family corporations, cooperatives, and partnerships; increased loan limits on many types of loans; set interest rates on farm ownership loans at the cost of borrowing to the government; and set a 5 percent rate for disaster and emergency loans. Comparable rates on new loans by the FLBs in the following three years were about double the FmHA disaster and emergency loan rate, averaging 9.2, 10.4, and 11.3 percent, respectively. The Agricultural Credit Act marked the beginning of the FmHA economic emergency loan program, which now accounts for about $5 billion or 2.5 percent of all farm credit outstanding. The favorable interest rates on emergency and disaster loans provided great incentive for larger farm operators to fall within those categories.

**Government Farm Credit Advances from Marginal to Major Source**

The increasing availability and easier terms of FmHA loans are reflected in the increasing number and amounts of loans outstanding. The number of active loans to farmers for all purposes totaled 241,790 in 1965 and 470,267 in 1970, then more than doubled during the 1970s to 1,167,006 and continued to rise during the first half of the 1980s (Table 8.3). From 7.2 percent of the nation's farmers in 1965, the number of FmHA active loans rose to 52.8 percent in 1983. This does not imply that more than half the nation's farmers are in debt to the FmHA. Many of the loans were made for rural nonfarm purposes and have little impact on farming operations. Also, one farmer may have both a farm ownership and a farm operating loan.

The fastest growth of all FmHA lending programs has been that of farm and economic emergency credit. The number of farmers borrowing under the farm emergency program (in designated disaster areas) rose sevenfold from 1970 to 1983, to about 5 percent of all farmers, while the economic emergency loans to hard-pressed farmers, which began in 1978, had risen to 2.6 percent of all farmers by 1983. These rapid increases in emergency credit occurred during a period of relatively high farm incomes and rapid growth in farm land values. For example, the number of farm emergency loans rose fivefold during the 1970s despite a rise in net income per farm from $4,800 to $9,225. Farm land values quadrupled. The sharp increase of government-subsidized emergency credit during a period

## Table 8.3
## ACTIVE FmHA LOANS

| Year | Loans to Individuals[1] | Number of Farm Loans by Type | | | |
|---|---|---|---|---|---|
| | | Farm Ownership | Farm Operating | Farm Emergency | Economic Emergency[2] |
| 1965 | 241,790 | 77,957 | 100,334 | 23,204 | — |
| 1970 | 470,267 | 101,904 | 89,039 | 18,536 | — |
| 1975 | 844,527 | 109,634 | 83,307 | 33,409 | — |
| 1980 | 1,167,006 | 118,424 | 87,073 | 93,102 | 61,225 |
| 1983 | 1,252,449 | 123,080 | 113,728 | 116,628 | 62,180 |
| | | FmHA Loans as % of U.S. Farms | | | |
| 1965 | 7.2 | 2.3 | 3.0 | 0.6 | — |
| 1970 | 15.9 | 3.5 | 3.0 | 0.6 | — |
| 1975 | 33.5 | 4.3 | 3.3 | 1.3 | — |
| 1980 | 48.0 | 4.9 | 3.6 | 3.8 | 2.5 |
| 1983 | 52.8 | 5.2 | 4.8 | 4.9 | 2.6 |

SOURCES: U.S. Department of Agriculture, Farmers Home Administration, *A Brief History of the Farmers Home Administration*, 1983 and 1984; and *Farmer Program Statistics*, 1939–77.
[1] Includes loans for rural and rental housing and water and waste.
[2] Program began in 1978.

of rising overall farm income and wealth suggests that much of the increase in such credit resulted from extremely favorable lending terms and more liberal interpretations of conditions that constitute emergencies rather than real deterioration in farm financial conditions.

The dollar value of government-subsidized credit to farmers remained at relatively modest levels for the two decades following the rapid growth of the 1930s. In 1940, such credit totaled $0.6 billion, 6 percent of total farm debt to all lenders. By 1960, FmHA credit, the major government lender, had risen to $1.1 billion; however, farm credit by private lenders rose even faster and the FmHA portion of the total declined to 4 percent (Tables 8.1 and 8.2). In 1960, subsidized government credit to farmers began to expand at a relatively rapid rate, rising to $2.2 billion in 1965. The higher rate of FmHA lending was maintained in the last half of the decade, but some deceleration occurred in the first half of the 1970s with the sharp increase in farm commodity prices and rising farm income. Nevertheless, by 1975 FmHA loans to farmers accounted for 6.8 percent of all farm real estate debt and 4.3 percent of non–real estate debt. Then FmHA credit again accelerated, far outstripping all other farm credit sources. From $5.2 billion in 1975, its loans rose to $19.5 billion in 1980 and in 1985 exceeded $27 billion. FmHA accounted for 9.9 percent of all real estate farm debt outstanding in 1985 and 20.8 percent of non–real estate farm debt (Tables 8.1 and 8.2).

As a result of the sharp increase of FmHA credit in recent years, subsidized government credit to farmers has become a leading farm credit source. It is no longer limited to the small struggling farmers who are attempting to retain a foothold in their inherited occupations; the large loans permitted in "disaster areas" and for "economic hardship" cases have opened this source of credit to a sizable portion of farm operators of all sizes.

### The Land Boom of the 1970s

The price of land is largely determined by the capitalized value of the flow of rents to owners. Investors evaluate the returns from land ownership against returns expected from alternative investments and purchase those resources that provide the highest rate of return. Highly subsidized FmHA credit (reducing the cost of capital) tends to increase the rental income stream to such borrowers and thereby have an impact on land values.

Hence the increasing liberality of FmHA lending on farmland in the 1970s led to spiraling land values, as did the easing of restrictions on Federal Land Bank lending after passage of the Farm Credit Act of 1971. The FLBs had been restricted to lending not more than 65 percent of the normal appraised value of farm real estate. The new law repealed this restriction and added emphasis on managerial ability, repayment capacity, and operational record. Borrowing of funds from the public by the FLBs also was eased somewhat as the new act permitted the issuance of a unified security for all banks in the system.

Coincident with the more liberal farm real estate lending policies of the FmHA and the FLBs, debt held by these agencies increased sharply. As shown in Table 8.1, the amount of farm real estate debt held by all major lenders rose sharply during the 1970s, largely reflecting a fourfold increase in land prices during the decade. However, the portion held by the FmHA and FLBs rose at a higher rate than did land values and almost double the rate of increase in such debt held by other major lenders. During the last half of the decade, when land values more than doubled, farm real estate debt held by other major lending groups—commercial banks, life insurance companies, individuals, and others—rose only 71 percent, while that held by the FmHA and FLBs rose 142 and 126 percent respectively (Table 8.4). Despite the leveling off of land values in 1980 and the downtrend from 1981 through 1985, loans by these agencies continued to increase.[2] Farm real estate debt held by the FLBs finally turned down in 1985—four years after the turndown in land prices—but in 1988 the amount held by FmHA remained near the peak levels reached in 1985.

By the mid-1970s FmHA credit had become available for almost any size farm, often at relatively low rates, and for almost any rural purpose. In addition to the reduced restrictions on FLB loans with passage of the 1971 Farm Credit Act, they could now be made for

[2]While FmHA lending on farmland rose at about the same rate as that of other lenders during the first half of the 1970s, it accelerated in the second half, when land prices rose sharply. This was a period when farming was relatively prosperous and such credit should have been held in check. Hence, it contributed to the excessive land values and the subsequent problems in farm real estate loan repayments.

## Table 8.4

CHANGE IN FARMLAND VALUE AND FARM REAL ESTATE DEBT
HELD BY SELECTED LENDERS (%)[1]

| Period | Farmland Value | FmHA Farm Real Estate Loans | FLB Loans | Other Farm Real Estate Loans |
|---|---|---|---|---|
| 1965–70 | 25 | 63 | 69 | 34 |
| 1970–75 | 90 | 38 | 124 | 46 |
| 1975–80 | 104 | 142 | 126 | 71 |
| 1980–85 | − 29 | 28 | 23 | − 2 |
| 1985–86 | − 9 | − 1 | − 16 | − 5 |

SOURCES: U.S. Department of Agriculture, *Economic Indicators of the Farm Sector: National Financial Summary*, 1986; and Table 8.1.
[1]Land value excludes operator household, but debt includes household.

a wider range of purposes, including the financing of farm-related businesses and the purchase of nonfarm rural homes. But their policies of setting rates charged borrowers on the basis of average cost of funds rather than marginal cost gave them a great advantage in rates from 1976 to 1981, when interest rates were rising. Consequently, the FLB rates were generally well below those of competitors, whereas following the interest rate peak in 1981 the FLB rates became less favorable to borrowers. Immediately following World War II, the FLBs and FmHA held 31.7 percent of the total farm real estate debt. In 1970, their combined percentage of 31.5 was little changed; however, their holdings had risen to 46.2 percent in 1980 and to 52.2 percent in 1985 (Table 8.1).

### The Wake of Farm Credit Excesses

The sharp upswing in land values in the 1970s and the equally sharp decline in the 1980s produced hardships that were exacerbated by the credit excesses stemming from the liberal lending policies of the FmHA and FLBs. Farmer borrowers who purchased land by obtaining large loans relative to land values in the late 1970s, when land prices were booming, found themselves with excessive debt in the 1980s; hence, failures were more frequent than would have occurred had the FmHA and the FLBs pursued more conservative lending policies like those of insurance companies, commercial banks, and others.

While sizable losses were realized by most major farm mortgage lenders, they were not as serious as those of the FmHA and FLBs. Numerous commercial banks in the Midwest failed during 1984–86 as a result of the poor performance of their farm loans. The failed banks, however, accounted for only a small percentage of the total banks in the area and an even smaller percentage of total bank loans and deposits, as the failures were concentrated among the smaller banks. These failures, plus farm loan losses by some surviving banks, were causes for concern by both the farm community and the Federal Deposit Insurance Corporation (FDIC), which insures all deposits of less than $100,000. However, the farm loan problem was a relatively small factor in the total banking system and was not the major source of FDIC losses. In addition to the FDIC losses, other losses included stockholders of the small banks and a few larger depositors whose deposits were not covered by FDIC insurance. Local communities were also inconvenienced by the loss of banking facilities.

Insurance companies and other farm mortgage lenders sustained similar types of entrepreneurial losses. These lenders (including commercial banks), however, entered loan agreements with an awareness of the risks and without any expectation of involuntary taxpayer assistance through government aid. Consequently, little taxpayer assistance—farm credit subsidies—has been received by these groups for their errors in judgment. An element of subsidy, however, developed in some farm loans. In a number of instances their farmer borrowers ceased to be creditworthy, and their non-performing loans were refinanced by the FmHA. Banks or other lenders were paid the face value of the debt, thereby preventing losses that would have otherwise occurred.

The subsidy element in most Farm Credit System loans (FLBs, FICBs, and BCs) has heretofore been relatively small since the retirement of the original government capital in 1968. As noted earlier, they paid the market rate on bonds, notes, and other borrowed funds for lending to farmers and charged farmers a rate high enough to cover operating costs and add to capital. But following their greater lending freedom authorized in the Farm Credit Act of 1971, the FCS banks and especially the FLBs began a rapid expansion of loans, reflecting overoptimism as to their future in the farm credit picture. The weakness in their policies, especially the FLBs, was delayed somewhat in surfacing as a result of their relatively strong capital position in the 1970s. Hence, their lending was maintained at a high rate for a number of years following the sharp downturn in land values in the early 1980s. By 1985, however, a number of FCS banks were reporting sizable losses, and in 1987 a bailout of the system became necessary.

The rescue bill for the FCS provided up to $4 billion in bailout funds, interest free, in the early years. A number of FLBs had asked for assistance under the act by early 1988, and others were in serious trouble with large portfolios of bad loans. Hence, the FCS has dropped back into the status of a government-subsidized credit supplier; taxpayers are called on to foot a portion of the bill for its unprofitable operations.[3] But it is not designed to remain regularly funded by government, whereas the FmHA will continue to provide subsidized credit to farmers.

**The Need for Subsidized Credit**

Despite the decline in the number of farms and the sharp increase in the number and volume of subsidized farm loans, calls for expanding the farm credit programs continue. The observed credit shortage for agriculture appears insatiable. One reason for this apparent anomaly of increased credit resources coexisting with a credit problem of rising intensity is that easy credit merely fuels the transformation of farming into a highly capital-intensive business. Since it is widely known that intensive use of fertilizer, chemical weed controls, large fields, and heavy mechanization can dramatically increase crop yields, the only factor slowing the make-over of farming from a labor-intensive to an investment-intensive structure is the cost of credit. As long as credit remains dear, smaller

[3]Some may contend that the bailout of FCS by the government was no different from the bailout of commercial banks by the Federal Deposit Insurance Corporation (FDIC) or the bailout of savings and loan associations by the Federal Savings and Loan Association Insurance Corporation (FSLIC). But there is a difference. The FDIC and FSLIC are insurance agencies supported by the commercial banks and savings and loan associations, respectively, rather than the taxpaying public. Costs of bailouts are thus borne by the industries and not by the public. Hence, their bailouts do not attract excessive resources into the industries as do bailouts of the FCS agencies.

farms that, say, still practice mechanical weed control, that use less fertilizer and mechanization and otherwise farm "gently," can compete. Once easy credit becomes available to some farmers, however, all must shift over to intensive, large-scale, capital-consuming cultivation in order to stay competitive.

Consequently, the addition of subsidized credit has been an important factor in changing many farming operations over to extremely expensive land-, chemical-, and credit-gobbling operations. Farming is a highly capitalized industry with total assets per farm averaging about $340,000 in 1985. Farms with sales of $40,000 to $100,000, which may be considered moderate-size commercial farms, had assets averaging $471,000 per farm (USDA 1985, 12–13, 80). Hence, cost of capital is a major cost of farming.

Differential access to subsidized credit can create strong advantages for the favored individuals. Assume, for example, that interest rates are 10 percent to nonsubsidized farmers and 5 percent to the FmHA-financed farmers. The cost of capital to the average nonsubsidized farmer in 1985 then totaled $47,000 for the farmer with $470,000 in assets, but only $23,500 for the subsidized farmer. Gross income per farm in 1985 for these farms averaged $76,000. This cost differential of about $30,000 per farm results in a major difference in average net income in favor of the credit-subsidized farmers. The program thus provides less efficient farmers a sufficient advantage in many instances to more than offset their lack of managerial skill.

As late as 1983, the FmHA pointed to a loss of 1 percent of principal advanced under the supervised loan program to farmers during its 47 years' experience as an indicator of the creditworthiness of its borrowers. This occurred, however, partly as a result of these borrowers' advantage in access to lower-cost credit and during a period of almost continuous increases in farm land prices. Farm land was a major security for many FmHA loans, and from 1940 to 1982, when most of the subsidized loans were made, the value of farm real estate in the United States rose at an average rate of 8.1 percent per year. At this rate of increase it would have been difficult to lose on farm real estate loans. The land could usually be sold for enough to liquidate the debt even if the farming enterprise failed. More recently, however, with the decline in farm land values, FmHA losses have begun to mount.

## Problems Created by Subsidized Credit

In addition to prolonging the agony of some less-efficient farmers who should have transferred to nonfarm occupations earlier, there are society-wide costs to subsidized farm credit. Credit is not an unlimited resource, so the channeling of additional funds into agriculture results in a smaller amount of credit and costlier terms both to farmers not eligible for the subsidies and to other sectors of the economy. Furthermore, to the extent that the FmHA takes operating losses, they are borne directly by the nation's taxpayers. The additional resources channeled to farms, such as farm equipment, fertilizer, other chemicals, seed, and energy supplies, as a result of the low-cost credit provide some marginal gains to food consumers and farm supply industries, but many of these potential gains are minimized by other government farm programs that tend to reduce acreage and production and to maintain farm commodity prices at above-market levels.

Some major weaknesses in FmHA programs have recently begun to fester and become more noticeable. With more than 100,000 less-efficient farmers established in agriculture through FmHA financing, the number of farmers in the low-income groups is much greater than it would have been without the program. Thus, the recent decline in overall farm income produced more casualties than those resulting from earlier declines.

Delinquency rates on FmHA farm ownership loans started to rise prior to 1980. With the decline of farm real estate values in the 1980s, delinquency rates zoomed, rising from 11 percent of the total at the end of 1980 to more than 30 percent at mid-1985 (Belongia and Carraro 1985, 26). While comparable data for 1985 are not available for other farm real estate lenders, the 1984 data indicate that repayment problems were much more severe among FmHA borrowers than among those borrowing elsewhere. For example, the Federal Land Banks, which now require a federal bailout, had farm real estate loan delinquencies of only 3.3 percent in mid-1984, while such delinquencies were in excess of 25 percent at FmHA.

Farm operating loan delinquencies at FmHA were even greater than for the farm ownership loans. These delinquencies rose from 12 percent of total loans in 1978 to 30 percent in 1981 and exceeded 55 percent in 1984 (Belongia and Carraro 1985, 26).

Although FmHA's stated losses have so far been relatively small, this largely reflects great forbearance in foreclosures by the agency. For example, at mid-1985 more than 45 percent of the volume of FmHA farm loans had been delinquent for more than four years. With a delinquency rate of 25 percent on farm ownership loans in 1984, chargeoffs totaled only 0.22 percent. In contrast, the Federal Land Banks with a delinquency rate of 3 percent had chargeoffs of 1.5 percent (Belongia and Carraro 1985, 26). These data indicate that major losses in real terms have already been realized by the FmHA and that its problems have only begun to surface.

*Nonsubsidized Farmers Lose Out*

Subsidized credit actually reduces the well-being of nonsubsidized farmers through its impact on farm production costs and product prices. It leads to increased usage of farm resources, and it causes more farmers to remain in farming than would have without such credit. Assuming that these effects are not counteracted by government production control measures, they add somewhat to total farm output and thereby exert a downward pressure on farm commodity prices and farm incomes.

The natural process whereby competition weeds out the less efficient and preserves the more efficient is altered by the introduction of subsidized credit to those farmers who are failing.[4] With a great advantage in capital cost through the use of such credit, even inefficient farmers can become successful. The overall competence of farm management suffers in the process. What's more, the successes of the subsidized farmers can lead to failure among the next group of farmers who theretofore were one step above the margin. Some in this group will find jobs elsewhere, and others will in turn apply for the subsidized credit and be able to remain farmers. The

[4]This analysis does not imply that all FmHA borrowers are less efficient than other farmers. However, since those not receiving emergency-type loans were usually ineligible for credit elsewhere, other lenders assume these loans to be risky, that is, the operation likely to fail and the lender to take losses or have the unpleasant duty of foreclosing. In some cases, highly qualified farm managers receiving FmHA loans but having insufficient assets to be eligible for conventional credit could have been successful by paying the higher interest rates in conventional loans. But this analysis assumes that conventional lenders made a reasonably accurate appraisal of the potential borrower and that most FmHA borrowers were less efficient than those eligible for conventional credit.

process thus continues until a major portion of all farm credit is extended at subsidized rates of interest.

*Effects on Private Lenders*

The FmHA argues that it is not a competitor of private lending agencies:

> FmHA programs operate as a supplement to credit made available by private lenders, not in competition with them, and as a helping hand to the capable and industrious family or community whose progress is blocked by lack of credit resources (USDA 1984, 9).

This view is shared by many farm credit analysts, by authors of farm finance textbooks, and even by the agricultural finance textbook of the American Institute of Banking, a section of the American Bankers Association, which states,

> Aside from special cases in which there may be a difference of opinion regarding the eligibility of specific borrowers for such loans, most lenders do not view the Farmers Home Administration as a competitor. They may welcome the presence of an agency to which they can refer promising farm borrowers who lack adequate credit standing for a bank loan (American Bankers Association 1969, 233).

Support for government-subsidized farm credit by private competitors reflects two factors. First is the view of many commercial bankers that the recipients of subsidized loans will eventually improve their financial condition and become profitable clients of the bank, both as borrowers and depositors. Second, credit analysis is not an exact science, and when errors creep in, losses by the private credit agencies are often made good by the FmHA. When a loan cannot be repaid, the FmHA often comes to the aid of the farmer and the lender by taking over the obligation. Private lenders thus often support federal credit measures because they rectify credit analysis mistakes and save the banks from losses.

Over the long run, however, subsidized credit crowds out private credit and reduces the opportunity for profits by suppliers. Although without FmHA help, some farmers would find credit unavailable, their land would not necessarily stand idle as a result. In many cases a farmer with stronger creditworthiness would purchase and farm such land, drawing on private credit to do so. Hence, a sizable fraction of FmHA credit outstanding would have been extended by the private sector, but to a different group of farm operators who possessed greater managerial talent and creditworthiness.

Few private lenders have been seriously damaged by FmHA competition since agriculture is a relatively small portion of the total economy. Most commercial banks, insurance companies, and individuals can find numerous nonfarm opportunities for lending and investing. The sharp decline in farm debt held by life insurance companies is indicative of such a move. Nevertheless, the credit market for these firms would have been somewhat greater in the absence of FmHA.

### Summary

Through the Farmers Home Administration, the federal government has become a major source of farm credit. Many farmers who would have otherwise failed have been able to continue farming with this assistance. Low-cost government credit provided them a major advantage in net income over farmers without such credit. The favorable impact of the subsidized credit, however, is more than offset by its unfavorable impact on taxpayers, other farmers, and users of scarce resources.

Instead of alleviating the problem of poverty in agriculture, such credit probably perpetuates the problem. Credit subsidies lower farm commodity prices and raise the cost of farm resources, especially land, thereby reducing net farm incomes. This tends to place the next group of farmers on the efficiency scale in the failure class. This process of replacing marginal farmers with otherwise submarginal ones results in a gradual reduction in the overall efficiency level of lower-income farm groups. Thus, despite major wealth transfers to the farm sector, losses within agriculture continue.

In addition, sizable net losses are realized in the nonfarm sector. Funds raised by the government to finance the program lead to increases in taxes, interest rates, and land prices. Losses are incurred by private lenders as a result of competition from government credit. These losses in the nonfarm sector are partly offset by somewhat lower food prices to consumers and increased sales to farmers by some resource suppliers. But the potential gains in lower-cost farm products are limited by government price support and production control programs.

What should be done? Subsidized farm credit is not compatible with an economic system that espouses equal opportunity for gain and loss. It largely rewards the inefficient at the expense of the efficient and the rest of the economy. Consequently, all FmHA farm purchase and emergency loan programs should be terminated. Farm operating credit subsidies should be phased out over a period of five years or less to provide fair competition in the farming industry.

The bailout of the Farm Credit System returns FLBs, FICBs, and BCs to near their original status as wards of the government. Also, despite the ill-advised banking policies followed in the late 1970s and early 1980s and the resulting failures, its stockholders were relieved of the loss borne by stockholders of most other failed firms. Losses were not realized for failure to chart sound banking courses, and since the means of disciplining was bypassed, the question arises—will ill-advised lending policies continue to prevail?

The solution is to break the FCS ties to government. If sufficient demand for FCS services exists to pay for their costs, the organization can prosper without the government props. The 1987 bailout, which allegedly made these agencies self-sustaining, should have provided for the eventual termination of all government ties. They could then operate as standard lending agencies. In this manner credit resources would be allocated so as to equalize returns at the margin and avoid the wastefulness resulting from the overcapitalization of agriculture.

# 9. The Dairy Program: Milking the Taxpayers

Headlines in major newspapers in 1986 pointed up the sometimes perverse effects of government actions to bolster dairy product prices. In response to the Department of Agriculture's Dairy Termination Program (DTP), which required the slaughter of a large number of dairy cattle, three beef cattle producers' groups filed a lawsuit claiming that the slaughter was enhancing the supply and reducing the price of beef (Karr, April 9, 1986). The buy-out program had originally been devised to reduce the output of dairy products and to increase the market price in order to maintain high support prices without excessive government purchases. The DTP authorized the USDA to purchase about 10 percent of the nation's dairy herds at a cost of $1.83 billion. Owners would retire from the dairy business by slaughtering the 1.6 million cattle in the herds (Karr, March 31, 1986). Spokesmen for the Cattlemen's Association alleged that beef cattle producers, who had no government price support program, lost $25 million in one week because of the beef price decline resulting from the kill-off.

The DTP followed a sharp buildup of milk cows on farms in response to high prices created by the government's dairy program. Rather than making the necessary reduction in price support levels, which would have reduced incentives to produce, the high-cost route was taken. The major losers, cattlemen notwithstanding, were taxpayers and consumers.

Milk cow numbers had risen to 11.18 million as of January 1986, up 3.5 percent from 1984. This reflected the rising profitability of the dairy industry. Milk prices were slightly lower in 1985 than in 1983 and 1984, but dairy feed costs declined even further. By the close of 1985 the government was finding it necessary to purchase about 10 percent of all dairy production in price support operations, at a cost of $2.2 billion (Table 9.1).

Buy-out bids in the DTP were accepted from 14,000 producers,

89

## Table 9.1

DAIRY PRODUCTS REMOVED FROM COMMERCIAL MARKETS BY
GOVERNMENT PURCHASES

| Year | Milk Equivalent (Billions of lb.)[1] | % of Production | Net Government Cost ($ Millions)[2] |
|------|------|------|------|
| 1949 | 2.5 | 2.2 | 188.1 |
| 1950 | 0.5 | 0.4 | −50.1 |
| 1951 | — | — | 9.1 |
| 1952 | 3.6 | 3.1 | 300.0 |
| 1953 | 11.3 | 9.4 | 474.4 |
| 1954 | 4.2 | 3.4 | 257.4 |
| 1955 | 5.1 | 4.1 | 284.2 |
| 1956 | 5.1 | 4.1 | 331.1 |
| 1957 | 6.8 | 5.5 | 360.0 |
| 1958 | 3.5 | 2.8 | 231.2 |
| 1959 | 3.4 | 2.9 | 218.2 |
| 1960 | 3.3 | 2.7 | 281.3 |
| 1961 | 11.2 | 8.9 | 612.0 |
| 1962 | 8.8 | 7.0 | 485.5 |
| 1963 | 7.5 | 6.0 | 379.1 |
| 1964 | 8.2 | 6.5 | 333.7 |
| 1965 | 5.7 | 4.6 | 68.6 |
| 1966 | 0.6 | 0.5 | 317.4 |
| 1967 | 7.4 | 6.2 | 364.2 |
| 1968 | 5.1 | 4.4 | 327.3 |
| 1969 | 4.5 | 3.9 | 290.9 |
| 1970 | 5.8 | 5.0 | 421.8 |
| 1971 | 7.3 | 6.2 | 338.2 |
| 1972 | 5.3 | 4.4 | 152.8 |
| 1973 | 2.2 | 1.9 | 70.9 |
| 1974 | 1.3 | 1.1 | 496.1 |
| 1975 | 2.0 | 1.7 | 76.5 |
| 1976 | 1.2 | 1.0 | 714.3 |
| 1977 | 6.1 | 5.0 | 451.4 |
| 1978 | 2.7 | 2.2 | 250.6 |
| 1979 | 2.1 | 1.7 | 1,279.8 |
| 1980 | 8.8 | 6.9 | 1,974.7 |
| 1981 | 12.9 | 9.7 | 2,239.2 |
| 1982 | 14.3 | 10.6 | 2,600.4 |
| 1983 | 16.8 | 12.0 | 1,594.6 |
| 1984 | 8.6 | 6.3 | 2,185.0 |
| 1985 | 13.2 | 9.2 | 2,200.0[3] |

SOURCES: U.S. Department of Agriculture, *Dairy Situation*, May 1971; *Dairy Situation and Outlook Report*, March 1986 and October 1986; *Dairy Situation and Outlook Yearbook*, July 1986.
[1]Calendar year for 1949; 15 months for 1950; April through March for 1951 through 1964; calendar year thereafter.
[2]Fiscal years beginning July 1 through 1976, October 1 thereafter.
[3]Estimated.

accounting for about 9 percent of total milk sales. Two-thirds of the dairymen selling out agreed to make their exit between April and August of 1986 and the remainder in the following 12 months. Farmers who contracted to leave the industry agreed to stay out for five years. A number of dairy farmers did very well indeed under the program. One hundred forty-six received more than $1 million each (Drinkard 1986). Given the possibility of a repeat performance of the DTP every five years, this group of producers could make going out of the dairy business a profitable enterprise.

## Dairy Price Supports

Like most other farm price support programs, the dairy program dates back to pre–New Deal years. Cartelized dairy marketing was given a major boost with passage of the Capper-Volstead Act in 1922, which exempted farm cooperative marketing organizations from some antitrust provisions. Dairy cooperatives were not only negotiating prices, weighing and testing milk for butterfat and bacteria count, and representing the political interests of the cooperative, but also processing cheese, butter, and other products. The Capper-Volstead Act required, however, that cooperatives avoid undue price increases (U.S. Senate Committee on Government Affairs 1978, 505).

Milk production cartels were given another boost by the New Deal in the early 1930s. Milk was included in the basic commodities eligible for price supports in the Agricultural Adjustment Act of 1933. It was viewed as being of sufficient importance that an improvement in returns to milk producers would have a favorable impact on the agricultural economy. However, no method was provided for restricting milk supplies comparable to the acreage reduction program for crops. A number of marketing agreements were made for pricing purposes, but they were soon replaced by a system of licenses with little restriction on production.

Drought relief and disease control programs in the early years of the AAA produced a small reduction of dairy cattle numbers. Also some farm price support was achieved through surplus removal purchases of butter and cheese used for relief activities. But a continuing program for dairy price enhancement was not established until passage of the Agricultural Marketing Agreement Act of 1937.

91

## Milk Marketing Orders

The stated goal of the Agricultural Marketing Agreement Act was to establish and maintain orderly marketing conditions for agricultural commodities (covered were milk, fruits, and vegetables). The act established the basic structure of today's milk marketing orders, which require that milk be classified according to its final use (fluid milk, processed milk such as cheese or ice cream, dried milk, and so forth) and that minimum and uniform prices be set in each of the nation's milk markets for each class of milk. Department of Agriculture representatives set the price of each class of milk in each of the milk markets, with prices varying from market to market and by season of the year.

The price of Class I milk (consumed as fluid milk) is set at a higher level than other classes, often resulting in an excess production of this class. Since drinking milk is highly perishable, little is shipped from one market to another. Consequently, local dairy farmers can exercise considerable power over the price of Class I milk in each of the local markets. The market power exercised by the cooperatives is greater and the price of milk generally higher in those markets where a single cooperative controls a major portion of the supply.

## Supply Controls

Although the Agricultural Marketing Agreements Act contained no specific method for controlling supply, its provisions have been used for supply control purposes. The most important of the supply control features is the classifying of milk and setting minimum prices for each class. The minimum price of Class I milk is generally negotiated at well above cost of production, and the quantity not sold as fluid milk goes into manufactured milk products. The fluid milk price thus usually exceeds the competitive price level. The gain to these producers, however, is offset to some extent by larger supplies and lower prices for the excess milk moving into processed uses.

State and local regulations ostensibly designed to protect public health by assuring high-quality drinking milk were frequently used to limit the free flow of milk from low-cost to high-cost producing areas. The Agricultural Marketing Agreements Act specifically prohibits any marketing order from limiting the marketing of U.S.–

produced milk or milk products. Nevertheless, factors such as alleged faulty labeling, reluctance to grant permits, different sanitation requirements, cost of sanitation permit fee, and state trade practice regulations often functioned as barriers to entry. These barriers were seldom necessary for the maintenance of high-quality milk and were used primarily to aid local producers in restricting supplies and maintaining higher prices.

Restrictions on the use of reconstituted milk also on occasion limit the interregional movement of dairy products. Federal milk marketing orders require that milk used in a drinking product must be sold at the Class I price; if the processor-distributor purchases powdered milk at cost and then adds water, the difference between Class I and Class II price must be paid into a pool to be distributed to dairy farmers (U.S. Senate Committee on Government Affairs 1978, 527–28). Hence the advantage of this lower-cost milk product is denied consumers.

Supply control of dairy products at the national level has consisted largely of import quotas. Quotas have been imposed on imports of dairy products since 1953. Imports are limited to a small percentage of annual U.S. consumption—generally less than 1 percent. Such quotas keep lower-priced foreign dairy products out of the United States and thereby increase the cost of such products to U.S. consumers.

**Mounting Surpluses**

While the organization of the government dairy program is more complex than that of other farm programs, the same general economic principles apply. Prices set by the government at above-market levels provide incentive for increased production and concurrently add to consumer costs, thereby reducing the quantity demanded. The Agricultural Act of 1949 made support prices mandatory not only on Class I milk, but on all milk and milk products (U.S. Department of Agriculture 1976, 7). All producers now became beneficiaries of the dairy price support programs. The price supports effectively placed a floor on the price of milk for manufacturing purposes, thereby encouraging even higher prices for Class I milk.

By agreeing to purchase all milk that cannot be sold in the market at the federally established support price, the government has maintained the price of milk at or above market levels each year since the supports began. As indicated in Table 9.1 the support price varied from levels that required only small government purchases to levels requiring the purchase of 10 percent or more of annual production. In 1950 and 1951, and from 1973 to 1976, support prices were maintained at or near market price levels, and very little purchasing of surplus milk by the government was required. In contrast, the purchase of 10.6 and 12.0 percent of annual production was necessary in 1982 and 1983 respectively.

Net government expenditures on products removed from the market were relatively low during the early years of the dairy program, but as with other support programs, costs have increased sharply over time. In the first three years of the price support program (1949–51) expenses averaged less than $50 million per year, or under 0.5 percent of net income to farm operators. From 1981 to 1985, however, the cost to taxpayers for removing surplus dairy products from the market averaged $2.2 billion per year, or about 8 percent of the nation's net farm income.

A number of attempts were made to relieve the surplus problem and at the same time to maintain price supports at above-market levels prior to the Dairy Termination Program. In 1983, a fee of 50 cents per hundred pounds was placed on milk to discourage production. This in effect lowered the support price by the same amount. The support price, however, remained high enough to encourage production, given the declining cost of dairy feed and the rising efficiency in the industry. Herds continued to expand (Belongia 1984).

As a consequence of continuing high price supports, farms remaining in the dairy business after the Dairy Termination Program are likely to continue to expand output, thereby largely offsetting the buy-out program. However, some reduction in the support price under the Food Security Act of 1985 (25 cents per cwt. effective January 1, 1987, and another 25 cents October 1, 1987) will lower somewhat the incentive to increase production.

## High Costs of the Dairy Program

One factor contributing to high dairy program costs is the highly perishable nature of milk. Unlike crops, milk cannot be stored by the CCC until reasonable opportunities arise for its liquidation. Class I milk is essentially nonstorable. Butter, cheese, and most manufactured dairy products are also perishable, and storage costs are high. Hence they must be liquidated over a relatively short period of time, and the government suffers a low recovery rate on the cost of price support purchases, even while these purchases have ballooned in the 1980s. As a consequence, direct costs to taxpayers for the dairy program totaled $2.6 billion in 1982 and averaged $2.2 billion from 1981 to 1985. Dairy price supports alone cost each household in the United States about $30 per year in taxes. In addition, consumers paid a higher price for dairy products than they would have without the program.

**Large Producers Gain Most**

An indication of the major gainers from the dairy price support program is found in the distribution of recent diversion payments in five leading milk-producing states (Table 9.2). In return for diverting up to 30 percent of their production from the market, 42,000 producers around the nation were paid approximately $955 million, or about $22,700 each, during a 15-month period in 1984 and early 1985. But three-fourths of the participants received only about 38 percent of the total payments, while the remaining quarter received 62 percent of the payments (*Economic Report of the President* 1986, 144).

*Table 9.2*

MILK DIVERSION PAYMENTS: TOP FIVE STATES, JANUARY 1984
TO APRIL 1985

| State | Total Payments ($ Millions) | Payments to $25,000 + Payees | | |
|---|---|---|---|---|
| | | Average Payment ($) | % of Payees | % of Dollar Amount |
| Wisconsin | 112.5 | 39,600 | 14.9 | 38.3 |
| California | 87.9 | 142,200 | 86.6 | 98.5 |
| Minnesota | 81.3 | 37,700 | 11.1 | 30.5 |
| Texas | 46.6 | 63,900 | 70.7 | 90.8 |
| Florida | 40.3 | 226,700 | 95.2 | 99.6 |
| U.S. Total | 955.3 | 57,100 | 24.9 | 62.3 |

SOURCE: *Economic Report of the President*, 1986, p. 145.

As indicated in Table 9.2, Wisconsin dairymen received the largest amount of payments ($112.5 million), but individuals receiving more than $25,000 accounted for only 38.3 percent of the state's total payments. In contrast, Florida dairymen received total payments of $40.3 million, but farmers receiving more than $25,000 in benefits consumed 99.6 percent of all Florida payments. Based on these data, 177 Florida dairymen receiving an average of $226,700 soaked up essentially all the payments in the state. Likewise, in California 608 dairymen with average payments of $142,200 received 98.5 percent of all payments.

While these diversion payments were made for a period of 16 months and are not net income, on an annualized basis they are very large sums, especially relative to the average taxpayer's income. They point to the possibility that the dairy program serves to transfer large amounts of funds from less wealthy taxpayers and milk consumers to more wealthy dairymen. In addition, they contribute to wastefulness through the inefficient use of valuable resources and the destruction of valuable products.

**Summary**

Government dairy programs started slowly, despite the fact that dairy farmers were better organized than most other commodity groups. Dairy farmers had formed into cooperatives during the 1920s and were given a boost toward cartel-type pricing with passage of the 1922 Capper-Volstead Act, which granted them the right to market dairy products collectively. The Agricultural Adjustment Act of 1933 designated dairy products as one of the basic commodities eligible for price supports, but little was done immediately to implement the objective of higher returns.

The establishment of milk marketing orders in the late 1930s gave rise to sharply higher prices for Class I (drinking) milk, but no method was provided for controlling production. This led to surpluses of Class I milk, which were diverted to manufacturing. The overall impact of the program on the consumer cost of dairy products was probably small, since the lower cost of manufactured dairy products partly offset the higher cost of drinking milk. There was also little impact on the average income of dairy farmers.

Conditions changed sharply with the direct price supports inaugurated in 1949. The industry now possessed great control over fluid milk via marketing orders, and surpluses resulting from price increases did not flow into processed products but were purchased directly by the government.

Despite its late start, the dairy program has recently become one of the most expensive and wasteful of all the farm programs. In recent years, about 10 percent of dairy production was removed from U.S. markets through government purchases, and disposed of at little or no return to the government. The direct cost of the program to taxpayers has averaged in excess of $2 billion per year, or the equivalent of 6 percent of total net income from farming. Furthermore, evidence indicates that the leading beneficiaries of the program were not low- to moderate-income family farmers but rather large dairies that are capable of operating in a competitive economy without government assistance.

Scarce resources used for the excess production of dairy products are essentially wasted. Without the program, somewhat fewer resources would be used for dairying, the supply of dairy products would be smaller, prices of dairy products to consumers would be somewhat lower, and output of other products somewhat higher as resources now steered toward dairy production would be used elsewhere. In addition, the cost to taxpayers would be reduced.[1]

[1]The high support prices for dairy products, like supports for other U.S. farm products and similar subsidies by other nations, have led to unwarranted increases in the size of the agricultural sectors and a maze of trade barriers to prevent the importing of competitive products. High domestic prices caused by the supports provide incentives to import similar goods. Governments thus have two choices: legislate barriers sufficiently restrictive to prevent the imports or purchase the imported products until the world price equals the domestic price. The latter may require very large government outlays; hence, most governments, including the United States, maintain the artificially high price supports by trade restrictions.

Thus, despite our espousal of free international trade policies following the New Deal of the 1930s and especially following World War II, this nation became increasingly restrictive in its trade barriers relative to dairy products. The 1935 amendment to the Agricultural Adjustment Act authorized the president to set quotas on imports of commodities if such importation tended to render ineffective or operated to hamper the program for raising the prices of farm products (Benedict 1955, 247).

The United States, although the world's major exporter of farm products and the most vocal proponent of free trade, until recently had consistently opposed the inclusion of moves toward agricultural free trade in the General Agreement on Trade and Tariffs (GATT). This opposition to liberal trade policies has surely influenced the Common Market and others to maintain similar barriers to agricultural trade (Johnson 1984, 736–37).

97

# 10. The Sugar Program: Sweet Deal for Producers

Government price assistance to producers of sugar crops differs from supports for other farm products. The cost advantage of sugar production outside the United States is so great that imports have historically accounted for a sizable portion of domestic use (Table 10.1). Until the late 1970s, subsidies to sugar cane and beet producers largely took the indirect form of tariffs and import restrictions.[1] Consequently, the costs of the sugar program were, until recently, hidden, borne largely by consumers of sugar and sugar products who pay the higher retail prices that it brings.

## An Overview of the Industry

Sugar cane and sugar beets each account for roughly 50 percent of total U.S. sugar production. Sugar cane is grown largely in Florida (47 percent), Hawaii (29 percent), Louisiana (20 percent), and Texas (3 percent). Sugar beets are more widespread, being harvested mainly in the Great Lakes, the Red River Valley, and the Great Plains areas. Thirteen states produce most sugar beets, with the largest output in Minnesota (22 percent), California (21 percent), Idaho (15 percent), North Dakota (11 percent), and Michigan (10 percent)." (Table 10.2).

[1] The sugar price support authority was expanded in the late 1970s to permit the secretary of agriculture to use additional price support measures, including loan/purchases and deficiency payments, in addition to the earlier tariffs and import quotas. In addition to price supports for sugar cane and beet producers, government subsidies are provided to the sugar refining industry. Sugar refiners have received both direct price supports and protection through the import quota system that set quotas on refined sugar entering the U.S. market. By limiting the supply of such imports, the price for domestically refined sugar was increased. The Agricultural Act of 1985 continued the program of price supports and import quotas on sugar. It carried over the existing system of giving price support loans to sugar processors "who agreed to share the support price with sugar cane and beet producers" (*Congressional Quarterly Almanac* 1985).

*Table 10.1*

U.S. Sugar Production, Use, and Imports (1,000 Tons Raw Value)

| Year | U.S. Production | | | Use (Military and Civilian) | Imports | % of Domestic Use Imported |
|------|------|------|-------|------|------|------|
| | Beet | Cane | Total | | | |
| 1970 | 3,401 | 2,416 | 5,817 | 11,163 | 5,296 | 47 |
| 1975 | 4,019 | 2,934 | 6,953 | 10,302 | 3,882 | 38 |
| 1980 | 3,149 | 2,728 | 5,877 | 11,150 | 4,881 | 44 |
| 1985 | 3,000 | 3,033 | 6,033 | 8,504 | 2,346 | 28 |
| 1986 | 3,414 | 3,281 | 6,695 | 8,637 | 1,685 | 20 |

SOURCES: U.S. Department of Agriculture, *Agricultural Statistics*, 1985, p. 85; and *Sugar and Sweetener: Situation and Outlook Yearbook*, June 1987, p. 19.

## Table 10.2

### U.S. SUGAR CROPS: ACREAGE, YIELD, AND PRODUCTION BY STATE, 1985

| | Acreage (Thousands of Acres) | Yield (Short Tons) | Production (Thousands of Short Tons) |
|---|---|---|---|
| Sugar cane (for sugar) | | | |
| Florida | 383 | 32.9 | 12,615 |
| Hawaii | 83 | 95.4 | 7,916 |
| Louisiana | 226 | 24.0 | 5,430 |
| Texas | 30 | 29.6 | 916 |
| U.S. Total | 723 | 37.2 | 26,877 |
| | | | |
| Sugar beets | | | |
| California | 203 | 23.5 | 4,771 |
| Idaho | 152 | 23.0 | 3,496 |
| Michigan | 118 | 19.7 | 2,325 |
| Minnesota | 276 | 18.4 | 5,088 |
| Montana | 43 | 19.0 | 811 |
| Nebraska | 53 | 23.1 | 1,229 |
| North Dakota | 144 | 16.8 | 2,423 |
| Ohio | 13 | 20.3 | 258 |
| Oregon | 12 | 27.0 | 319 |
| Texas | 37 | 22.5 | 833 |
| Wyoming | 49 | 21.0 | 1,037 |
| U.S. Total | 1,103 | 20.5 | 22,636 |

SOURCE: U.S. Department of Agriculture, *Sugar and Sweetener: Situation and Outlook Report*, September 1985.

Sugar farms range in size from small to gigantic. Sugar cane plantations in Florida, for instance, averaged 2,199 acres in 1978. Hawaii was second in size of farms and California third. Sugar beet farms are closer to the average size of all U.S. farms, but overall large farms dominate the sugar industry.

U.S. use of sugar derived from cane and beets reached a peak of 11.5 million tons in 1972 and by 1986 had declined to 8.6 million tons (Table 10.1). Per capita consumption dropped more than 30 percent during the period. Total caloric sweetener use has continued to increase, however, rising from 12.7 million short tons in 1975 to 15.5 million in 1986 (Table 10.3). Per capita consumption of all sweeteners rose from 124.2 to 146.8 pounds during this period.

Corn products such as high fructose corn syrup, glucose, and dextrose were the beneficiaries of this shift, rising from 3 million tons, dry basis, in 1975 to 8 million tons in 1986 (Table 10.3). At the latter date, the use of corn sweeteners had surpassed the combined total of cane and beet sugar. Per capita consumption of refined sugar declined from 89.2 to 60.9 pounds during 1975–86 while that of corn sweeteners rose from 27.5 to 66.2 pounds. Beverage makers are the primary users of corn sweeteners.

## Aid to Sugar Producers, 1789–1986

Use of the power of the federal government to enhance sugar prices and producer incomes dates back to the nation's first tariff, adopted in 1789, which specified duties on sugar (Benedict 1953, 45). Since almost all the nation's sugar supply at that time was imported, this action raised the price of sugar to domestic producers about the amount of the duty. While the early tariffs were allegedly designed to provide revenue for the young nation rather than to transfer wealth from consumers to producers, the result was the same. A few domestic sugar producers gained from the duties, and consumers paid higher prices.

By 1816, the protection of domestic producers from the "evils" of foreign competition had become a major rallying point, and there was agitation for tariff increases. Further duties were levied on sugar. Since then, with the exception of a short period, 1890–94, the nation has maintained gradually increasing duties on sugar. With the exception of some special measures during World War I involving direct government purchases of sugar from producers, import duties were the chief means of government aid to sugar producers until passage of the Agricultural Adjustment Act and other New Deal legislation of the 1930s.

The Jones-Costigan Act of 1934 added sugar beets and sugar cane to the list of basic crops for which the secretary of agriculture was authorized to make rental and other payments for supply control and income-support purposes. A critical feature of the act, however, was its imposition of sugar import quotas on foreign nations at a time when the nation was otherwise espousing free trade through

## Table 10.3
## U.S. CONSUMPTION OF CALORIC SWEETENERS
### (MILLIONS OF SHORT TONS)

| Year | Refined Sugar | High-Fructose Syrup | Corn Sweeteners Glucose (Dry Basis) | Dextrose | Total | Honey | Edible Syrups | Total |
|------|------|------|------|------|------|------|------|------|
| 1975 | 9.6 | 0.5 | 1.9 | 0.5 | 3.0 | 0.1 | — | 12.7 |
| 1980 | 9.5 | 2.2 | 2.0 | 0.4 | 4.6 | 0.1 | — | 14.2 |
| 1985 | 7.6 | 5.2 | 2.2 | 0.4 | 7.8 | 0.1 | — | 15.5 |
| 1986 | 7.4 | 5.4 | 2.2 | 0.4 | 8.0 | 0.1 | — | 15.5 |

SOURCES: U.S. Department of Agriculture, *Agricultural Statistics*; and *Sugar and Sweetener: Situation and Outlook Report,* September 1986.

reciprocal trade agreements.[2] More restrictive legislation occurred with passage of the Sugar Act of 1948, amended in 1971, 1977, and 1986.

Prior to 1956, Cuba and the Philippines together accounted for about 96 percent of U.S. sugar imports. Following the advent of Castro's regime, Cuba in the early 1960s, was denied the highly valuable rights to market sugar in the United States. The Cuban quotas were dispersed among other nations, largely less-developed countries in the tropics. Quota allotments were by then quite valuable. Imports were strictly limited, and domestic sugar prices were now well isolated from world conditions. The secretary of agriculture controlled domestic production, established import quotas, and generally set prices.

## Impact of the Sugar Program

Americans have paid above-world prices for sugar during most of the nation's history. Throughout most of those years, especially after the early 1950s, domestic sugar production rose rapidly in response to high prices. During the three decades from 1950 to 1980, production of sugar crops in the United States, including beets, cane, and maple syrup, rose 68 percent.[3]

The extent of subsidization provided sugar producers is indicated by the difference in New York and Caribbean wholesale prices for

[2]Evidence of the capricious manner in which quotas were awarded to the various sugar exporting nations is the long list of lobbyists they hired to maintain or obtain larger quotas. The quotas were so valuable (that is, the price for sugar in the United States was so far above the world price) that even small nations with little prospect for obtaining larger quotas found it necessary to hire lobbyists in efforts to maintain or increase their quota awards.

During an investigation of the influence of lobbyists on the quota system in 1971, the chairman of the Senate Committee on Finance, Sen. Russell Long (D–La.), remarked, "I might say those who hired lobbyists did very well. Argentina did not hire a lobbyist and just got the worst of it in all respects" (Johnson 1974, 34).

[3]Measures of the comparative advantage of producing sugar in the Caribbean countries versus the United States are difficult to determine. Under competitive free trade conditions the producer prices in the United States and abroad would approach equality, and comparative advantage would be measured by the direction and quantity of shipments. The desire for additional exports by the exporting nations as indicated by their lobbyists and testimony before Congress points to a major comparative advantage of Caribbean sugar producers. For an excellent discussion of this subject, see Johnson (1974, chapter 5).

raw cane sugar as shown in Table 10.4. Since 1981 the price differential between U.S. and world sugar has increased sharply, indicating greater protection of domestic producers from competition abroad. In each of the four years from 1982 to 1985, U.S. prices were more than double the world price. Indeed, in 1985 the New York wholesale price was five times the world price. A major factor in this relative price rise was tightened import restrictions. In 1973, more than 5 million tons of sugar were permitted to enter the United States under the quota system (Johnson 1974, 13). By 1980, imports totaled only 4.9 million tons and in 1986 they were just 1.7 million tons. In 1987 we imported less sugar than we did 75 years ago.

*Table 10.4*

AVERAGE PRICE OF SUGAR ABROAD AND IN THE UNITED STATES
(¢ PER POUND)

| Year | Wholesale Price, Raw Cane Sugar | | U.S. Retail Price, Granulated Sugar |
|------|-----------------------|----------|---------------------|
| | Caribbean Ports | New York | |
| 1969 | 3.37 | 7.8 | 12.4 |
| 1970 | 3.75 | 8.1 | 13.0 |
| 1971 | 4.52 | 8.5 | 13.6 |
| 1972 | 7.43 | 9.1 | 13.9 |
| 1973 | 9.61 | 10.3 | 15.1 |
| 1974 | 29.99 | 29.5 | 32.3 |
| 1975 | 20.49 | 22.5 | 37.2 |
| 1976 | 11.58 | 13.3 | 24.0 |
| 1977 | 8.11 | 11.0 | 21.6 |
| 1978 | 7.82 | 13.9 | 23.7 |
| 1979 | 9.66 | 15.6 | 24.9 |
| 1980 | 29.02 | 30.11 | 42.7 |
| 1981 | 16.93 | 19.73 | 40.0 |
| 1982 | 8.42 | 19.92 | 34.3 |
| 1983 | 8.49 | 22.04 | 36.2 |
| 1984 | 5.18 | 21.74 | 36.3 |
| 1985 | 4.04 | 20.34 | 35.3 |

SOURCE: U.S. Department of Agriculture, *Agricultural Statistics*, 1984; and *Sugar and Sweetener: Situation and Outlook Report*, September 1986.

Not only do quotas provide a means for isolating the United States from the world sugar market, they are also used to discipline quota recipients for failure to support U.S. foreign policies. In this respect they are similar to foreign aid. By permitting the entry of 347,000 tons of sugar from the Philippines in 1985, for instance, to be sold for prices $326 per ton above the world price, the U.S. government effectively granted the Philippines $100 million in extra income. These changes can take place at the whim of U.S. policy-makers without any additional expense to U.S. consumers.

This system of using government-imposed prices (a tax) on U.S. consumers to purchase friends abroad was turned around to punish Cuba following establishment of the Castro regime, with results that have been less than satisfactory. At that time Cuba's sugar quota was withdrawn, and it has not been renewed. Beginning with the 1985–86 quota year, restrictions were further tightened on Cuba-produced sugar with the ruling that no import quota would be allocated to a country that is a net importer of sugar unless it can prove that it does not import and then export Cuban sugar to the United States (U.S. Department of Agriculture 1986 [March], 12). Such actions tend to ignore the fungible nature of sugar in world markets.

**Demise of the Sugar Industry**

Recently, the cartel-like structure of the U.S. sugar industry has begun to disintegrate. Like the dairy farmers who fought a losing battle against soybean and cotton producers in the 1940s and 1950s in an attempt to prohibit the use of low-cost oleomargarine as a substitute for higher-priced butter, sugar producers have discovered a dangerous domestic competitor in the massive corn production industry.

In 1985 an estimated 450 million bushels of corn, 5.2 percent of all production, was milled to produce sweeteners. Corn sweetener use exceeded U.S. sugar use for the first time (Table 10.5). Small quantities of corn sweeteners, largely syrups, have been used throughout this century, but prior to the 1970s they were not generally viewed as a major competitor in the sugar market. As late as 1975, corn sweeteners accounted for only 24 percent of the nation's total caloric sweetener consumption. By 1986, however, they represented 52 percent of the market. (Lost in the 1986 furor over Coca-Cola's attempt to change its classic formula was the fact that the

## Table 10.5
### U.S. PRODUCTION, IMPORTS, AND CONSUMPTION OF CALORIC SWEETENERS
### (MILLIONS OF SHORT TONS)

| Year | Refined Sugar[1] Production[3] | Imports[3] | Consumption | Corn Sweeteners Consumption | Total[2] Consumption |
|---|---|---|---|---|---|
| 1975 | 5.9 | 3.6 | 9.6 | 3.0 | 12.7 |
| 1976 | 6.4 | 4.4 | 10.2 | 3.2 | 13.6 |
| 1977 | 5.7 | 5.7 | 10.4 | 3.4 | 14.0 |
| 1978 | 5.2 | 4.4 | 10.2 | 3.8 | 14.1 |
| 1979 | 5.4 | 4.7 | 10.1 | 4.1 | 14.3 |
| 1980 | 5.4 | 4.2 | 9.5 | 4.6 | 14.2 |
| 1981 | 5.8 | 4.7 | 9.1 | 5.1 | 14.4 |
| 1982 | 5.5 | 2.8 | 8.6 | 5.6 | 14.3 |
| 1983 | 5.3 | 3.0 | 8.3 | 6.1 | 14.6 |
| 1984 | 5.5 | 3.3 | 8.0 | 6.8 | 15.0 |
| 1985 | 5.6 | 2.7 | 7.6 | 8.0 | 15.7 |
| 1986 | 5.8 | 2.1 | 7.4 | 8.1 | 15.7 |

SOURCES: U.S. Department of Agriculture, *Agricultural Statistics*, 1984, p. 85; and *Sugar and Sweetener: Situation and Outlook Yearbook*, June 1987, pp. 19, 22, and 23.

[1]Consumption does not equal production plus imports because of changes in inventories and a small amount of exports.

[2]Includes small quantities of honey and edible syrups.

[3]One hundred pounds of raw sugar equals 93.46 pounds of refined sugar.

formula *did* quietly change: most Coke is now produced with high fructose corn syrup, not sugar.)

This sharp growth can be attributed largely to low corn sweetener prices relative to sugar prices. The season-average price of corn rose from $2.35 per bushel in 1975–76 to $2.80 in 1980–81, an increase of 19 percent, while sugar prices rose from an average of 17.9 cents per pound in 1975–76 to 24.9 cents per pound in 1980–81, an increase of 39 percent. Since 1980, corn sweetener prices have remained well below the price of an equivalent amount of refined sugar, pointing to further growth in this sugar substitute (Table 10.6).

In addition to fueling the shift to domestic sugar substitutes, the growing differential between U.S. and world sugar prices provides great incentive for increased imports of sugar substitutes not covered by quotas and tariffs. In 1985, imports of dextrose rose 12 percent from the 1984 level and totaled 2.5 times that of 1983. Other sweeteners imported in sharply rising quantities include high fructose corn syrup, maple syrup, honey, liquid sugar, and molasses (U.S. Department of Agriculture, 1986 [March], 12).

Up until now, the declines in sugar consumption have come mostly out of imports. Sugar imports in 1986 were 1.7 million tons, down from 4.9 million tons in 1980 and 5.3 million in 1970

---

*Table 10.6*

PRICES OF REFINED SUGAR AND HIGH-FRUCTOSE CORN SYRUP (HFCS)
(¢ PER LB., DRY BASIS, CHICAGO-WEST MARKET)

| Year | Refined Sugar Price | HFCS-42 Price | HFCS-42 % of Sugar Price | HFCS-55 Price | HFCS-55 % of Sugar Price |
|------|------|------|------|------|------|
| 1981 | 28.26 | 21.47 | 76.0 | 23.59 | 83.5 |
| 1982 | 27.62 | 14.30 | 51.8 | 18.81 | 68.1 |
| 1983 | 26.09 | 18.64 | 71.4 | 21.60 | 82.8 |
| 1984 | 25.66 | 19.94 | 77.7 | 22.70 | 88.5 |
| 1985 | 23.18 | 17.75 | 76.6 | 20.03 | 86.4 |
| 1986[1] | 23.31 | 17.06 | 73.2 | 19.22 | 82.5 |

SOURCE: U.S. Department of Agriculture, *Sugar and Sweetener: Situation and Outlook Report,* September 1986.
[1]Average of first and second quarters.

(Table 10.1). If current patterns continue, it will soon be necessary to end sugar imports altogether in order to maintain current prices to U.S. producers. And soon after, regular reductions will have to be made in domestic sugar production.

Most sugar-exporting nations are underdeveloped. More than two-thirds of all U.S. sugar imports come from the Dominican Republic, Guatemala, Brazil, Columbia, Peru, the Philippines, El Salvador, and Panama, nations we profess to support in our international trade policies. By closing off one of their most profitable export markets, we have dealt these countries a severe economic blow. We have also caused many South American sugar growers to turn to marijuana cultivation.

### New Legislation, Old Problems

While the 1985 Omnibus Farm Bill was hailed as a cost-cutting measure and a move toward greater production freedom, it may prove to be neither for the sugar industry. It continued the existing price support loans, import quotas and tariff duties. It authorized the secretary of agriculture to make annual adjustments in support prices based on changes in the general price level. It required the president to use all available authority to operate the program at "no cost," that is, to impose strict limits on imports in order to assure high domestic prices without the need for government price support intervention.

All the failings of past sugar programs were contained in the 1985 act. Large price support subsidies continue to underwrite inefficient domestic production during a period of rapid decline in sugar consumption. Quotas on imports further restrict trade with less-developed sugar-exporting nations even while the United States professes concern for their development, calls for more capitalism in developing countries, and exhorts other nations to follow a liberal trade policy. The sugar program contributes to price inflation by raising sugar costs. It perpetuates useless government economic controls during an era of supposed deregulation.

Of even greater concern to sugar producers and legislators, the program will probably collapse within the next decade or two. As shown in Tables 10.1 and 10.4, domestic sugar prices have been maintained at very high levels relative to world prices since 1980. Domestic consumption has declined 23 percent during the past six years and production was maintained only at the expense of sharply reduced imports. This pattern cannot be continued. Yet the new act contains nothing to alleviate or reverse the deterioration of the sugar market. This time it is not the powerless growers in small foreign countries who are providing the competition for domestic sugar producers but a massive number of domestic corn growers. The substitution of corn-based sweeteners for overpriced sugar will no doubt continue, eventually at the expense of domestic sugar producers.

The heart of the problem with the sugar industry is the government's maintaining of artificially high prices. As shown in Table 10.1, U.S. sugar production was 14 percent greater in 1986 than in 1980. This occurred during a period when domestic sugar prices increased to five times that of Caribbean sugar prices (Table 10.4). In a free market this drastic shift in prices would have led to a major reduction in U.S. sugar production and a sharp increase in imports. Import quotas, however, prevented this from happening, so instead consumers shifted to domestic corn sweeteners and imported sugar substitutes.

The wide gap between U.S. and world sugar prices led to a similar differential in sugar substitute prices. Consequently, producers of Canada's much lower-priced corn sweeteners found the U.S. market attractive, as did others, and imports of sugar substitutes rose sharply. (Tariffs on sugar substitutes are fairly low.) In addition, a sizable increase occurred in imports of sugar-containing products, which also fall outside the quota system. In 1985, in excess of 40,000 tons of such products containing 29,500 tons of sugar were sold for domestic consumption in the United States. The bulk consisted of gelatin mixes and flavored syrups (U.S. Department of Agriculture 1986 [September], 14). An even bigger threat to the domestic sugar industry than this small seepage of sugar substitute imports through our trade barriers is the rise of domestically produced corn sweeteners. Since it is an excellent replacement for sugar in its major uses, corn sweetener could rapidly undercut U.S. sugar production if it continues to enjoy a considerable price advantage.

### Summary

Early aid to sugar producers was limited to tariff duties on imports, which assured producers higher-than-world prices for their product. This began almost two centuries ago, allegedly for the purpose of raising revenue. But protection of domestic producers from foreign competition soon became the leading issue. Up until the New Deal, a gradually increasing set of tariffs and duties was used to restrict sugar imports. The Agricultural Adjustment Act of 1933 went one step further and made sugar a price-supported crop. In 1934 a quota system further reduced imports.

Sugar program proponents, however, were not content with a moderate amount of protection, and the restrictions were tightened more and more over the years, widening the spread between domestic and world prices. In recent years domestic sugar prices have risen to three or four times world levels. Well protected, U.S. production has grown. Consumers, meanwhile, have been forced to pay much more for sugar than necessary.

The sugar cartel's effectiveness began to decline when strong domestic competitors for the sugar market appeared in the 1970s. The leading substitutes for sugar are corn sweeteners. Because of resistance from the nation's massive number of corn growers, sugar producers have so far been unable to exclude corn sweeteners from the U.S. market as they did sugar imports. In recent years, substitution of corn sweetening for sugar has proceeded to the point where corn sweeteners now predominate.

To date, nearly all of the decline in sugar consumption has been absorbed by reducing imports. While voting foreign aid funds to assist less-developed sugar-producing nations and espousing self-help programs for them, we have actually reduced their economic independence by denying them open access to the U.S. sugar market. Soon, however, sugar imports will have disappeared altogether. Then, overpriced sugar's continuing loss of market share to corn sweeteners will cause serious problems for long-sheltered domestic producers.

# 11. The High-Cost Way to Aid Low-Income Farmers

The stated objectives of this country's massive farm programs have been to raise farm commodity prices and incomes. As discussed in chapter 2, the early programs were designed to increase the purchasing power of farmers through commodity price supports and production controls. They were largely concerned with the well-being of farm people in general rather than remedial measures for specific economic groups within a widely diverse population. Although an enormous amount of taxpayers' money is channeled into the programs, at no time have policy discussions focused on whose incomes within the farm sector are being supported. From most of the program debates it could be assumed that American agriculture is a homogeneous industry, especially with respect to incomes and wealth of the participants, and that transfers from taxpayers to farmers will automatically amount to assistance to hard-pressed farmers.[1]

In truth, farmers are a highly diverse group. Some are landlords only, owning farms strictly as an investment. Others are owner-operators supplying most of the capital, land, and labor used in the enterprise. Still others are tenants, sharecroppers, or day laborers.

Incomes of these people, both within the various tenure groups and from one group to another, are highly variable. In 1985, 27,000 farms in the nation had sales of $500,000 or more, with net incomes averaging $640,010 (Table 11.1). At the upper extreme of this income group 144 dairy farmers in 1986 received government checks of more than $1 million each in the Dairy Termination Program (Kieckhefer 1987). Also in 1986, the prince of Liechtenstein and

---

[1]An exception to this assumption of homogeneity occurred following the direct payments programs in the 1970s, when news media and taxpayers began to observe the wide diversity in size of payments to farmers, and especially the huge checks received by larger farmers. The debate initiated by the wide variation in the size of payments continues.

## Table 11.1
### FARM INCOME BY SIZE OF FARM, 1985[1]

| Sales Class | Farms | | Gross Cash Income | | Average Income ($) | | Net as % of Gross |
|---|---|---|---|---|---|---|---|
| | Number (Thousands) | % of Total | $ Millions | % of Total | Gross | Net | |
| Under $40,000 | 1,638 | 72 | 16,064 | 10.3 | 14,603 | -1,635 | — |
| $40,000 to $99,999 | 323 | 14 | 24,468 | 15.7 | 80,534 | 6,566 | 8.2 |
| $100,000 to $249,999 | 221 | 10 | 39,383 | 25.2 | 184,449 | 36,660 | 19.9 |
| $250,000 to $499,999 | 66 | 3 | 25,987 | 16.6 | 401,473 | 99,661 | 24.8 |
| $500,000 and over | 27 | 1 | 50,266 | 32.2 | 1,852,614 | 640,010 | 34.5 |
| All farms | 2,275 | 100 | 156,167 | 100.0 | 73,616 | 13,811 | 18.3 |

SOURCE: U.S. Department of Agriculture, *Economic Indicators of the Farm Sector: National Financial Summary*, 1985, pp. 14, 42, 49.

[1]Includes operator households, before inventory adjustment.

his business partner, owners of Texas farmland, were paid more than $2 million in federal aid to distressed farmers (*Commercial Appeal* 1986). At the other extreme, 1,638,000 farmers in 1985 had sales of less than $40,000 each and negative average net incomes. Most of those operators, however, held other jobs from which they earned their living.[2] Farm laborers, who also fall in the lower income class, are generally paid less than their urban counterparts, but much of the difference can be accounted for by differences in education and living costs.

## The Winners

How are the economic benefits of government farm programs distributed among this diverse farm population? In contrast to the generally accepted view, higher prices for farm commodities and other program benefits do not necessarily improve in a significant way the status of the relatively low-income people who constitute a major portion of the farm population. There are basic reasons for this. A breakdown of farm income into its constituent parts points to the means by which the gains are distributed and provides clues as to the identity of the chief gainers.

Owners of land, labor, and capital fare differently from changes in the price of farm commodities. For example, an increase in prospective farm income will increase the demand for hired laborers. Agriculture, however, accounts for a small percentage of the nation's hired labor force, and the supply is highly elastic. Over the longer run the increased number of workers demanded can be obtained with little increase in wages. Thus, there will be overall gains in the returns to all farm workers as a result of the larger number of workers employed but little gain to each worker.[3] Consequently,

[2]Official statistics count as farms any place that sells or could sell as of June 1, $1,000 worth of agricultural products. Hence, such occupations as mail carriers, drivers of school buses, school teaching, and all types of shift work that permit some time off for farming may allow one to be classified as a farmer. Off-farm income of operator households of farms with sales of less than $40,000 averaged $20,741 in 1985. In comparison, such income averaged $10,347 for those farms with sales of $40,000 to $99,999, and $10,742 for those with sales of $100,000 to $499,999.

[3]The supply of farm labor is highly elastic with respect to wage rates; for example, a small increase in farm wages provides sufficient incentive for many laborers to want farm employment. Rising demand for farm workers thus largely affects the number employed in agriculture rather than wages per worker.

current farm programs will have little effect in raising the income of farm families whose resources consist largely of their own labor. That eliminates about 30 percent of those persons now working on farms.

Farm tenants who operate farms but supply only their labor and equipment likewise receive little long-run gain from the programs. Resources supplied by this group are relatively elastic, with small increases in prices of farm commodities providing incentive for large increases in the quantity supplied. Tenant labor, like other farm labor, tends to adjust in response to price changes, and any immediate gains resulting from farm programs are soon diluted by larger tenant operating costs and a greater number of tenants.

There is one farm resource that, unlike farm labor and other inputs, cannot be increased in a relatively short period of time with little increase in cost per unit. Farmland is the one farm resource that is relatively inelastic in supply. New acres can be brought into production through reclamation, irrigation, drainage, and so forth, but at a relatively high cost. Consequently, an increase in prices of farm commodities grown on existing acres will result in increased rents to owners of existing land.

Such gains are a one-time-only gain, as land values will soon be bid up to reflect the expected higher returns. The artificially high prices of farm commodities resulting from government programs are thereby transmitted primarily to land values, which move to artificially higher levels reflecting the higher anticipated rental returns. Following a new stabilized rental level, there are no further gains to landowners unless benefits are further increased. But owners of land remain vitally interested in government price supports because they are necessary to *maintain* the inflated land values. A removal of supports will result in a sharp decline in the wealth of landowners.

The steady augmentation of price support and commodity income programs during the late 1950s, the 1960s, and the 1970s, plus the expanded export market in the latter decade, caused land prices to rise sharply as the higher returns were increasingly capitalized into land values. But by the early 1980s farmland values had been bid up beyond what returns to land would justify. In the mid-1980s land purchasers and farm real estate credit suppliers experienced losses as land prices declined to more realistic levels.[4]

[4]For example, assume that the stream of rental income from corn producing land

Despite the downward adjustment in land prices in the mid-1980s, they probably remain above levels consistent with free-market pricing of farm commodities. Hence, large landowners remain program proponents, as the subsidies continue to serve as a brake to the decline in land values.

## Benefit Distribution

Following the implementation of target pricing and increased direct government payments to farmers in the 1970s, the politically sensitive disparity of program benefits to individual farmers was widely revealed. Payments to high-income farmers were limited somewhat in 1970 when a cap ($55,000 at that time) was placed on the amount paid to any producer. Largely reflecting this cap, in 1982 the 324,000 farms with sales of $100,000 or more received only 48.3 percent of all direct government payments, well below their 67.5 percent share of gross farm income (Table 11.2). But by 1983, with the arrival of the Payment-in-Kind program, the proportion of government payments received by these high-income farmers had returned to 66.7 percent, almost equal to their 68.7 percent of gross farm income. The proportion of payments to this group inched up further in 1985, to 68.8 percent.

While direct government payments to farmers are only a small portion of the net social costs of the farm programs, the distribution of these payments, when they became public information, revealed to the public that they were not based on poverty or "need."[5] There are two generally accepted measures of poverty: the official poverty line established by the Office of Management and Budget and the earned income tax credit threshold for those entitled to refundable

---

rises at 5 percent per year as a result of the farm programs, the real rate of interest is 4 percent and rental returns at the beginning of the programs are $50 per acre, and the capitalized land value (the income stream of $50 per year to the owner) is $\frac{\$50}{0.04}$ or $1,250. Income to land will rise to $52.50 ($50 × 1.05) the second year with rising government aid, and land values will increase to $1,312.50 $\left(\frac{\$52.50}{0.04}\right)$. As the rising supports continue over a long period of time, expectations of permanency are built into the process, and any tendency to stabilize or reduce the rate of growth in the programs leads to major declines in land prices, as occurred in the 1980s.

[5]Social costs are those costs incurred by consumers and taxpayers in excess of the gains by the beneficiaries of the programs, that is, the net loss to the nation.

## Table 11.2
### DIRECT GOVERNMENT PAYMENTS TO FARMERS BY SALES CLASS[1]

| | $500,000 and Over | $250,000 to $499,999 | $100,000 to $249,999 | $40,000 to $99,999 | Under $40,000 | All Farms |
|---|---|---|---|---|---|---|
| **Total Payments ($ Millions)** | | | | | | |
| 1982 | 293 | 387 | 1,005 | 1,065 | 742 | 3,492 |
| 1983 | 1,415 | 1,769 | 3,025 | 1,994 | 1,092 | 9,295 |
| 1984 | 1,005 | 1,430 | 3,119 | 1,897 | 980 | 8,430 |
| 1985 | 1,024 | 1,437 | 2,834 | 1,677 | 732 | 7,704 |
| **Distribution of Payments (%)** | | | | | | |
| 1982 | 8.4 | 11.1 | 28.8 | 30.5 | 21.2 | 100 |
| 1983 | 15.2 | 19.0 | 32.5 | 21.5 | 11.7 | 100 |
| 1984 | 11.9 | 17.0 | 37.0 | 22.5 | 11.6 | 100 |
| 1985 | 13.3 | 18.7 | 36.8 | 21.8 | 9.5 | 100 |
| **Average Payments ($)** | | | | | | |
| 1982 | 9,829 | 6,160 | 4,341 | 2,987 | 431 | 1,455 |
| 1983 | 48,632 | 27,509 | 13,209 | 5,748 | 642 | 3,922 |
| 1984 | 35,559 | 21,877 | 13,837 | 5,650 | 586 | 3,621 |
| 1985 | 37,499 | 21,783 | 12,845 | 5,193 | 447 | 3,387 |
| **Distribution of Gross Income (%)** | | | | | | |
| 1982 | 29.7 | 14.0 | 23.8 | 16.5 | 16.0 | 100 |
| 1983 | 29.8 | 14.8 | 24.1 | 16.1 | 15.3 | 100 |
| 1984 | 30.2 | 15.2 | 24.0 | 15.6 | 15.1 | 100 |
| 1985 | 30.2 | 15.8 | 24.3 | 15.5 | 14.3 | 100 |

SOURCE: U.S. Department of Agriculture, *Economic Indicators of the Farm Sector: National Financial Summary*, 1985, pp. 46, 52.

[1]Includes payments to eligible nonoperating landlords.

payments of up to $550 under income-tax legislation. The poverty line for a family of four in 1985 was $10,989, and the earned income credit line was $11,000.

Judged by these measures, federal farm programs tend to operate counter to the generally accepted view of welfare benefits. The distribution of direct government payments in 1985 reveals that more than two-thirds of the total went to the 314,000 farms with sales in excess of $100,000. The payments averaged $37,499 per farm with sales in excess of $500,000; $21,783 per farm with sales of $250,000 to $499,999; and $12,845 per farm with sales of $100,000 to $249,999. Just 31 percent of the payments went to farms with sales of less than $100,000, and payments averaged $5,193 for farms with sales of $40,000 to $99,999 and $447 for those with sales under $40,000 (Table 11.2).

**The Losers**

One method of estimating the cost to taxpayers of the farm program is to deduct from total USDA expenditures outlays for research, extension services, and plant, animal, and food protection, plus a portion of food and nutrition program expenses. One can view the remainder as a subsidy to the industry. Such subsidy costs (Table 11.3) totaled $33.9 billion in 1985, or 75 percent of the USDA budget.

*Table 11.3*

FEDERAL OUTLAYS FOR FARM INCOME MAINTENANCE, 1985

| Program | Amount ($ Billions) |
|---|---|
| Farm income stabilization (off budget) | 1.2 |
| Farm income stabilization (on budget) | 18.3 |
| Food and nutrition (0.5% of total) | 9.3 |
| Conservation and land management[1] | 1.0 |
| FmHA[2] rural housing insurance fund | 2.3 |
| FmHA agricultural credit insurance fund | 1.2 |
| FmHA rural development insurance fund | 0.6 |
| Total | 33.9 |

SOURCE: Based on data in U.S. Department of Commerce, Bureau of the Census, *Statistical Abstract of the United States*, 1986, p. 307.
[1]Excludes water resource programs.
[2]Farmers Home Administration.

It appears that more than 10 percent of that total went to farms with gross incomes in excess of $500,000. Almost 70 percent went to farms with gross incomes of $100,000 or more.

While the federal farm programs were designed to transfer income from the more affluent nonfarm sectors of the economy to downtrodden farmers, the ultimate result has often been the opposite.[6] Although total per capita income of the ultimate gainers from the programs is not available, it is apparent that the programs on average result in a transfer of wealth from the less affluent to the more affluent.[7]

What's more, the long-run beneficiaries of our farm program likely number no more than 267,000 large landowning farm operators, plus some nonoperator landlords and a small number of people whose jobs and salaries are predicated on the programs. The total gainers from the programs are probably fewer than 500,000 families. In contrast, the losers number about 99 percent of the nation's households, including all taxpayers and consumers, who face higher taxes and food prices.

### Rising Direct Costs

Despite the fact that government assistance to agriculture has increased relative to farm product sales and net farm income in almost every decade since the Great Depression, rising to more than total net farm income in recent years, proponents of the programs continue to urge increased assistance. Newspaper headlines cry out "Farm Credit Official Calls for Federal Help" (*Commercial Appeal* 1987), "Sugar Producers Lobbying Congress to Keep Their Share of U.S. Imports" (*Lachica* 1986), and "U.S.'s Commodity Certificate Program Is Failing to Ease Major Farm Problems" (*Brown* 1987). Farm failures and foreclosures are the highest since the 1930s.

---

[6]As will be discussed later, gross and net farm incomes are not satisfactory measures of poverty in agriculture. Off-farm income accounts for a major portion of total family income of those farmers in the smaller gross income class. Nevertheless, as indicated by average net income per farm, which totals $36,660 for those farms in the $100,000 to $249,999 sales class, most farm poverty (family income of $10,000 or less) will likely occur in the 1,961,000 farms with sales of less than $100,000 per year.

[7]Many of the large landowners purchased their farms after the program benefits had been capitalized into the land and did not realize increased wealth resulting from the programs. However, they would realize losses if the programs were discontinued. Hence, they are usually strong program proponents.

There is an explanation for both aid and failures being up. Any initial injection of price support subsidies will result in short-run income gains. To maintain the same effect over time, however, it becomes necessary to steadily increase the size of the subsidy. Over a period of two to four years, the increased returns that the price supports made possible draw new resources and new people into the industry. Prices of farm products will then decline again, and if the improved returns are to be maintained, subsidies must be increased once more. The whole cycle then repeats itself. The simultaneous existence of large government expenditures on farm programs in the mid-1980s with relatively small impact on net farm income (realized government losses in some years exceeded net farm income and USDA expenditures were two to three times net farm income) confirms this principle of ineffectual subsidy ratcheting.

Conversely, a withdrawal of price supports would immediately cause commodity prices and farm incomes to decrease. Returns to all factors (land and variable inputs) would decline. Land prices would drop, and variable resource prices (labor, outlays for machinery, equipment, chemicals, fertilizer, and so forth) would move toward their value in nonfarm uses. However, within four or five years farm commodity prices and farm incomes would gradually return to pre-support or competitive levels. Ultimately, it is society-wide economic conditions, the relation of demand to fixed resources, and the allure of alternative occupations that determine the returns on farming, not government price setting.

### Social Costs of Farm Programs

In addition to redistributing income inequitably, farm programs contribute to economic waste and sizable social losses. The dollar gains by a few large landowners and others are well below the dollar losses of consumers and taxpayers. While attempts to measure the extent of the social costs (losses to taxpayers and consumers minus gains to producers and others) are little more than conjectural, two estimates have been made that are rough guides to students of the topic.

Economist Bruce Gardner has estimated that the total costs to consumers and taxpayers of U.S. farm programs exceeded total producer gains by about $1.5 billion in 1978–79 (Gardner 1981,

121

72–74). His conservative analysis excluded some losses incurred through conflicting programs, such as production-enhancing subsidies to irrigation and soil enrichment at the same time as acreage controls to reduce production. Likewise, Gardner excluded the costs of peripheral programs such as food stamps, even though they are justified in part by their contribution to farm product demand.

A similar analysis of the farm programs' social costs was made by the president's Council of Economic Advisers in 1987 (Table 11.4). Again, major peripheral program costs were not included. For example, the estimates omitted the costs to farmers, manufacturers, and others incurred in political lobbying for the programs. In one reasonable scenario these estimates showed a producer gain of $20 billion per year and consumer and taxpayer cost of about $25.2 billion, for a net loss of $5.2 billion.

In addition to their specific omissions, both of these analyses were limited to short-run effects. Over time, as has been argued here, the early gains to farm labor, equipment, and other farm

*Table 11.4*

ANNUAL GAINS AND LOSSES FROM FARM INCOME-SUPPORT PROGRAMS UNDER 1985 FOOD SECURITY ACT ($ BILLIONS)

| Commodity | Consumer Loss | Taxpayer Cost[1] | Producer Gain | Net Loss |
|---|---|---|---|---|
| Corn | 0.5–1.1 | 10.5 | 10.4–10.9 | 0.6–0.7 |
| Sugar I[3] | 1.8–2.5 | 0 | 1.5–1.7 | 0.3–0.7 |
| Sugar II[3] | 1.1–1.8 | 0 | 1.0–1.4 | 0.1–0.4 |
| Milk | 1.6–3.1 | 1.0 | 1.5–2.4 | 1.1–1.7 |
| Cotton | (2) | 2.1 | 1.2–1.6 | 0.5–0.9 |
| Wheat | 0.1–0.3 | 4.7 | 3.3–3.6 | 1.4–1.5 |
| Rice | 0.02–0.06 | 1.1 | 0.8–1.1 | 0.06–0.32 |
| Peanuts | 0.2–0.4 | 0 | 0.15–0.40 | 0–0.05 |
| Tobacco | 0.4–0.7 | 0.1 | 0.1–0.2 | 0.4–0.6 |

SOURCE: *Economic Report of the President* (Washington: GPO, 1987), p. 159.
[1]Includes CCC expenses after cost recovery.
[2]Less than $50 million.
[3]Case I assumes that U.S. policies do not affect world sugar prices. Case II takes into account the fact that U.S. policies reduce world sugar prices. The value of sugar import restrictions to those exporters who have access to the U.S. market (that is, the value of quota rents) is $250 million.

resources will be diluted by movement of new resources into farming. Presented in Table 11.5 are more inclusive estimates of social costs of farm programs, including some of the peripheral, non-direct expenses, and beginning with the consumer cost and tax-payer loss estimates reported by the Council of Economic Advisers. About one-quarter of subsidized farm credit (0.25 × $11 billion) must be considered a loss. Most of the $0.5 billion spent for soil and water conservation, which tends to increase production, can also be considered wasted, given the offsetting acreage reduction programs for reducing farm output. These and some other losses to consumers in wasted resources are arbitrarily placed at $10 billion.

As indicated earlier, the primary long-run beneficiaries of farm subsidies are landowners. Only crude estimates are available as to total rent on farmland. According to the 1982 Census of Agriculture, about 40 percent of the nation's farmland was rented. Net rent received by nonoperator landlords in 1985 totaled $7.4 billion. This suggests that all U.S. farmland had a rental-equivalent value of about $18.5 billion.[8] For analytical purposes, it is assumed that about one-third of that total, or $6.2 billion, can be attributed to the effect of farm programs. There are other beneficiaries of farm programs: for instance, some USDA employees, others whose jobs depend on the programs, and some suppliers of farm resources. Including their interests, benefits from farm subsidies may total $8 billion.

Based on this analysis, the full social costs of farm programs may have exceeded $30 billion in 1985 rather than the $6 billion upper limit estimate of the Council of Economic Advisers. This is more in line with the results of Gardner when he includes such peripheral farm programs as food stamps. Gardner argued that, in truth, the entire $6 billion of direct farm price and income support transfers to farmers that took place in 1978–79 should be considered a loss, though the USDA reported just $3.2 billion worth as a loss. Given the increased direct transfer payments to farmers since 1978–79, that would be consistent with a $20 to $25 billion social loss in the mid-1980s.

## Alternative Methods of Fighting Farm Poverty

Prior to coming to grips with the problem of farm poverty it is useful to ask, Is it worse than elsewhere in the economy, and, if

[8]In 1985, total U.S. farm real estate value excluding the operator's household was $559.6 billion, and the $18.5 billion represents a net rental return of 3.3 percent.

123

## Table 11.5
POTENTIAL SOCIAL COST OF FARM PROGRAMS IN THE LONG RUN (5 YEARS AND OVER) ($ BILLIONS)

| Source of Gain or Loss | Consumer Loss | Taxpayer Cost | Producer and Others' Gain | Net Loss |
|---|---|---|---|---|
| Commodity programs[1] | 4.4 | 19.5 | | |
| Peripheral programs—food and nutrition[2] | -7.5 | 9.4 | | |
| Financing farmers and rural development[3] | — | 2.7 | | |
| Conservation of land and water resources | — | 0.5 | | |
| Inefficient allocation of resources between farm and nonfarm uses[4] | 10.0 | — | | |
| Total | 6.9 | 32.1 | 8.0[5] | 31.0 |

SOURCE: Based on data in *Economic Report of the President*, p. 159.
[1]Summary of Table 11.4 using midpoints of data and Case II for sugar.
[2]One-half of $18.8 billion outlay allocated to farm programs in 1986; assumes stamps valued at 80 percent by recipients.
[3]One-fourth of $11.0 billion outlay in 1986.
[4]Excesses in agriculture include both labor and capital that would have been used in nonfarm production.
[5]One-third of estimated farmland rental plus $1 billion for other gainers.

124

so, by how much? Fortunately, some data are available on this question, as shown in Table 11.6. On the basis of a poverty line of $10,989 for a family of four in 1985, about 17 percent of all farm families were poor in 1985. That is somewhat higher than the 11 percent of all U.S. families falling below the poverty line. These estimates, however, are based on money income and may overstate the disadvantage of farm families. Considering nonmoney perquisites, such as lower-cost housing, garden plots, lower community expenses, and so forth, farm families may fare better than it appears.

In any case, if the elimination of poverty in agriculture is the primary objective of the farm programs, it can be done at a fraction of current costs. The poverty deficit of about $2.0 billion for all farm families combined, as shown in Table 11.6, could be eliminated by writing checks totaling this amount to these families. That is only 6 percent of the above estimate of possible social costs of the present farm program. A sudden dismantling of existing subsidies would, it is true, increase the poverty deficit for farm families in the short run. Even if it doubled, however, farm poverty elimination could be achieved for only $3.9 billion.

It is sometimes argued that farmers and family farms are a stabilizing influence on free democratic institutions and worth preserving on those grounds alone. If so, this also could be achieved at a major savings in farm program costs. One possible method is to place every farmer in the nation (wealthy and poor) on the federal payroll until death, or until he reaches 70 years of age, at an inflation-adjusted salary equal to 50 percent of his average net farm income for the three years 1984–86. No new farmers could be added to this favored list, so any fresh entrants to the farming occupation would do so only on the basis of expected rewards in a competitive environment. All present farm programs would be dismantled immediately and government costs for them reduced to zero.

The cost of this program in 1987 would have been $15.4 billion, well below the USDA budget and less than the estimated social cost of the programs. Furthermore, since the number of subsidized farmers will decline annually and reach zero after about 40 years, the costs of the program will similarly decline. In the meantime, these favored farmers plus any others willing to practice unsubsidized agriculture could produce farm products in a competitive environment, to the great benefit of consumers, taxpayers, and the

### Table 11.6

**ALL U.S. FAMILIES AND FARM FAMILIES BY INCOME AND ESTIMATED POVERTY DEFICIT, 1985**

| Income class | All Families Number (Thousands) | Farm Families Number (Thousands) | Farm Families Deficit per Family[1] ($) | Farm Families Deficit for Class ($ Thousands) |
|---|---|---|---|---|
| Under $2,500 | 1,226 | 114 | 9,739 | 1,110,246 |
| $2,500 to $4,999 | 1,834 | 49 | 7,239 | 354,711 |
| $5,000 to $7,499 | 2,685 | 57 | 4,739 | 270,123 |
| $7,500 to $9,999 | 2,744 | 92 | 2,239 | 205,988 |
| $10,000 to $12,499 | 3,292 | 116 | −261 | 22,698[2] |
| $12,500 and over | 51,777 | 1,134 | — | — |
| Total | 63,558 | 1,562 | — | 1,963,766 |
| Percentage below poverty line ($10,989) | 11.2 | 17.0 | | |
| Average income ($) | 32,944 | 25,695 | | |

SOURCE: U.S. Department of Commerce, Bureau of the Census, *Current Population Reports: Consumer Income*, series P-60, no. 154, 1985.

[1] $10,989 poverty line index for 1985 less midpoint of class.

[2] Interpolating within this class indicates that 45,900 families fell below the poverty line and had an average deficit of $495.

export trade. Resources in the farm sector would adjust to market demands, rather than being maintained at artificially inflated levels as a result of the massive government income transfers to the industry.

This proposal should assure all current farmers an income at least equal to current income. Even during the tumultuous short-run adjustment of the farming industry to competitive markets, it is unlikely that net farm income would fall below 50 percent of the 1984–86 level. With their government salary supplement, most farmers would be better off even in the face of reduced net income from farming. And this would occur with less expense and waste of resources than under current practices.

## Why Tax the Poor to Enrich the Wealthy?

The anomaly of our present farm program is the willingness of free citizens to pay heavily for a system that primarily helps a small number of more wealthy farmers. To paraphrase Churchill, seldom has a government taxed so many for the benefit of so few. Not only are the programs economically inefficient, they run counter to the basic charitable instincts of most people. The only explanation for this is that, as pointed out by economist George Stigler, the election of obliging candidates is of much greater concern to an industry or group seeking special favors than to the typical voter. Although the beneficiaries of the U.S. farm program are few in number, their financial interests are considerable. The average voter, on the other hand, has little reason to inform himself as to the merits of our current agricultural practices. With no natural interest group to curb excesses, it is excess—extreme excess—that has resulted.

## Dismantling the Farm Programs

If current government farm subsidies were ended, there would be large immediate benefits. Taxpayer gains alone would likely average $400 or more per family. In addition to our domestic gains, U.S. agricultural liberalization would contribute enormously toward increased free international trade. The United States could then unambiguously push for open trade, which would result in increased production of optimally priced goods and services in all nations.

Two additional gains would likely follow the elimination of the programs. First, economic growth in the less-developed nations

127

would likely accelerate, as much of their exports consist of farm commodities where trade barriers are most restrictive. Greater freedom of trade for these products would provide these nations with more foreign exchange to purchase goods and services from the wealthier nations, thereby reducing their need for foreign aid. Second, the elimination of the programs would likewise eliminate a major cause of discord among the wealthier nations. Trade barriers, government production subsidies, and dumping of farm products create considerable ill will among Western nations.

Although no wholly pleasant solution to our current agricultural problems is available to policymakers, it appears the programs may be reaching a turning point. The public increasingly seems aware of the demerits of the current program structure. A move toward market-determined prices for farm commodities and resources would seem to be inevitable.

Obviously, national policies should avoid overly abrupt changes, as that would result in sharp declines in agricultural returns for a year or two until sizable adjustments have been made. A gradual reduction of the programs, publicly announced and adhered to, would likely cause the least disturbance. If confidence is placed in the pronouncements, appropriate plans can be made by the affected resource managers (including small farm operators and farm labor) at an early stage, thereby reducing the hardships resulting from the transfers. A five-year program might be appropriate for phasing out current subsidies and controls and returning to a competitive agriculture.

If we fail to make the move toward freedom in agriculture, the political search for means of increasing farm income will likely continue at ever-increasing costs to taxpayers and consumers, resulting in further regulation and more highly inefficient, centralized decision making. Accumulating problems and snowballing costs—that is the unmistakable legacy of more than 50 years of government manipulation of American agriculture.

## Summary

The power of the federal government has been used for more than half a century to transfer wealth from taxpayers and consumers to a small group of landowners and agricultural suppliers via the farm program. In many cases, these amount to reverse transfers: subsidies by the less affluent for the more affluent.

Despite the high cost of our current agricultural programs, they contain an internal growth mechanism. The various instruments of U.S. farm policy—acreage controls, nonrecourse commodity loans, export subsidies, dairy cattle buyouts, tariffs, import quotas, price supports, government land rental programs, direct payments to producers, and others—all have the effect of increasing the returns to farmers. In so doing, however, they increase the incentive to produce. Over the longer run, then, they are self-defeating, because they encourage the use of new and excessive resources in the industry.

In the presence of these new resources, returns are once again diluted, and subsidies must be ratcheted up again just to return to the earlier income standard. Repeated several times, this cycle can consume enormous amounts of government aid without significantly improving farmer welfare.

The one agricultural input that cannot easily be increased, however, is land. Because the supply of good land is relatively inelastic, rents and land values will be permanently enhanced so long as government programs to raise farm incomes remain in force. Major landowners—few of whom are low-income—are therefore the segment of the farm economy that most clearly profits from government subsidies.

Even in the short run, more than two-thirds of all direct payments to farmers go to individuals with $100,000 or more of annual gross sales. Attacked in this inefficient way, our programs to reduce farm poverty now have totaled net costs to society of up to $30 billion. If the government just sent checks directly to those farm families who fall beneath the poverty line, sufficient in size to bring them out of poverty, the total cost would be only about $4 billion.

Even if the goal of farm programs is defined more broadly as "the preservation of family farming as an institution of social value," the job could be achieved much more cheaply. All families now farming could be so maintained for life for about half of current costs.

Aside from saving money, dismantling current farm programs would have other benefits. It could spark a significant new move toward freer world trade. That would contribute enormously toward economic development in the Third World. And it would ease serious tensions among Western nations over agricultural subsidies.

An end to the distortions of our current system could be brought about without undue turmoil over a period of several years. But it will require political will. Otherwise, program costs and warped effects on agricultural output will continue to rise.

# References

American Bankers Association, American Institute of Banking. 1969. *Agricultural Finance*.

Belongia, Michael T. "The Dairy Price Support Program: A Study of Misdirected Incentives." *Review* (February 1984), Federal Reserve Bank of St. Louis.

Belongia, Michael T., and Kenneth C. Carraro. "The Status of Farm Lenders: An Assessment of Eighth District and National Trends." *Review* (October 1985), Federal Reserve Bank of St. Louis.

Benedict, Murray R. *Farm Policies of the United States, 1790–1950*. New York: Twentieth Century Fund, 1953.

———. *Can We Solve the Farm Problem?* New York: Twentieth Century Fund, 1955.

Benson, Ezra Taft. *Farmers at the Crossroads*. New York: Devin Adair, 1956.

———. *Freedom to Farm*. Garden City, N.Y.: Doubleday, 1960.

———. *Crossfire: The Eight Years with Eisenhower*. Garden City, N.Y.: Doubleday, 1962.

Black, John D. *Economics for Agriculture*. Cambridge: Harvard University Press, 1959.

Brown, Jean Marie. "U.S.'s Commodity Certificate Program Is Failing to Ease Major Farm Problems." *Wall Street Journal*, February 9, 1987.

*Commercial Appeal (Memphis)*, December 11, 1986. "Royalty, Partners Get Princely Sum in Government Aid."

———. March 25, 1987. "Farm Credit Official Calls for Federal Help."

*Congressional Quarterly Almanac*. "Farm Bill Granted a Limited Win on All Sides." 99th Cong., 1st sess., 1985.

Drinkard, Jim. "U.S. Pays Millions to Some Dairies." *Commercial Appeal*, December 24, 1986.

*Economic Report of the President*, 1986.

Galbraith, John Kenneth. "The Case for Agriculture." In *Contemporary Readings in Agricultural Economics*. Edited by Harold G. Halcrow. New York: Prentice-Hall, 1955.

Gardner, Bruce L. *The Governing of Agriculture*. Lawrence: The Regents Press of Kansas, 1981.

Hadwiger, Don F. *Federal Wheat Commodity Programs*. Ames: Iowa State University Press, 1970.

Johnson, D. Gale. *The Sugar Program, Large Costs and Small Benefits*. Washington, D.C.: American Enterprise Institute for Public Policy Research, 1974.

————. "Domestic Agricultural Policy in an International Environment: Effects of Other Countries' Policies on the United States." *American Journal of Agricultural Economics* (September 1984).

Karr, Albert R. "U.S. to Pay Dairy Farmers $1.83 Billion to Quit Business, Reducing Milk Surplus." *Wall Street Journal*, March 31, 1986.

————. "Cattle Raisers Sue in Effort to Halt Slaughter of Cows." *Wall Street Journal*, April 9, 1986.

Kieckhefer, E. W. "Farm Policy Expected to Draw Further Debate." *Commercial Appeal*, February 16, 1987.

Lachica, Eduardo. "Sugar Producers Lobbying Congress to Keep Their Share of U.S. Imports." *Wall Street Journal*, October 9, 1986.

Legge, Alexander. "Policy and Program of the Federal Farm Board." *Journal of Farm Economics*, 7, no. 1 (January 1930).

Luttrell, Clifton B. "Farm Price Supports at Cost of Production." *Review* (December 1977), Federal Reserve Bank of St. Louis.

————. "Good Intentions, Cheap Food and Counterpart Funds." *Review* (November 1982), Federal Reserve Bank of St. Louis.

Meltzer, Allan H. "Monetary and Other Explanations of the Start of the Great Depression." *Journal of Monetary Economics* (November 1976).

Nourse, E. G. "The Outlook for Agriculture." *Journal of Farm Economics* 9, no. 1 (January 1927).

Schapsmeier, Edward L., and Frederick H. Schapsmeier. *Henry A. Wallace of Iowa: The Agrarian Years, 1910–1940.* Ames: Iowa State University Press, 1968.

Stigler, George J. "The Theory of Economic Regulation." *Bell Journal of Economics and Management Science* (Spring 1971).

Taylor, Henry C., and Ann Dewees Taylor. *The Story of Agricultural Economics in the United States, 1840–1932.* Ames: Iowa State College Press, 1952.

Thompson, John G. "Causes of the Cityward Movement." *Journal of Farm Economics* 4, no. 1 (January 1922).

U.S. Department of Agriculture. Agricultural Stabilization and Conservation Service. *Farm Commodity and Related Programs.* Agricultural Handbook no. 345. 1976.

————. *Chronological Landmarks in American Agriculture.* Agriculture Information Bulletin no. 425. Rev. 1980.

————. *Economic Indicators of the Farm Sector, National Financial Summary.* 1985.

————. *Dairy Situation and Outlook Yearbook.* March, June, July 1986.

————. *Economic Indicators of the Farm Sector: Production and Efficiency Statistics.* Various years.

U.S. Department of Agriculture, Farmers Home Administration. *Yearbook of Agriculture*. 1935.

———*A Brief History of the Farmers Home Administration*. 1984.

———*Farm Commodity and Related Programs*. Agricultural Handbook no. 345. 1976.

———. *Sugar and Sweetener: Outlook and Situation Report*. March 1986.

———. *Sugar and Sweetener: Outlook and Situation Report*. September 1986.

U.S. Department of Treasury, Internal Revenue Service. *Your Federal Income Tax*. Publication 17. Rev. November 1986.

U.S. Senate. Appropriations Committee on Agriculture. *Hearings on Distribution of Government-owned Wheat and Cotton*. 1932.

———. Committee on Government Affairs. Appendix to vol. 7. *Framework for Regulation, Study of Federal Regulation*. December 1978.

———. Committee on Agriculture, Nutrition and Forestry. *The Food Stamp Program: History, Description, Issues, and Options*. Committee print, April 1985.

*U.S. Statutes at Large*. "An Act to Establish a Federal Farm Board—." H.R. 1, June 15, 1929.

———. 48:31 "An Act to Relieve the Existing Economic Emergency by Increasing Agricultural Purchasing Power—." H.R. 3835, May 12, 1933.

# Appendix

Data presented in Appendix Tables A-1 and A-2 may differ substantially from program data found elsewhere. In some cases the differences are the result of discrepancies in time periods covered (fiscal years, calendar years, months included in the growing season, and so forth).

In other cases, differences occur because of what is included or excluded in each category. For example, agricultural losses incurred under P.L. 480 shipments are usually listed in State or Defense Department budgets.

Support and market prices for some major farm commodities shown in Table A-4 reveal only a portion of the divergence of the support price from the free-market price of the commodity. With the predominance of U.S. products in many world markets, any influence that the programs had on domestic supply and demand would likewise be reflected in world supply and demand and in prices.

## Table A-1

### USDA OUTLAYS AS PERCENTAGE OF FEDERAL GOVERNMENT OUTLAYS AND NET FARM INCOME

| Year | USDA Outlays | Federal Outlays[1] | Net Farm Income | USDA Outlays as % of Federal Outlays | USDA Outlays as % of Net Farm Income |
|------|------|------|------|------|------|
| | ($ Billions) | | | | |
| 1932 | 0.3 | 4.7 | 2.0 | 6 | 15 |
| 1933 | 0.3 | 4.6 | 2.6 | 7 | 12 |
| 1934 | 0.6 | 6.6 | 2.9 | 9 | 21 |
| 1935 | 1.2 | 6.5 | 5.3 | 18 | 23 |
| 1936 | 0.9 | 8.5 | 4.3 | 11 | 21 |
| 1937 | 1.2 | 7.8 | 6.0 | 15 | 20 |
| 1938 | 0.9 | 6.8 | 4.4 | 13 | 20 |
| 1939 | 1.4 | 9.1 | 4.4 | 15 | 32 |
| 1940 | 1.4 | 9.5 | 4.5 | 15 | 31 |
| 1941 | 1.5 | 13.7 | 6.5 | 11 | 23 |
| 1942 | 2.1 | 35.1 | 9.9 | 6 | 21 |
| 1943 | 2.6 | 78.6 | 11.7 | 3 | 22 |
| 1944 | 2.8 | 91.3 | 11.7 | 3 | 24 |
| 1945 | 2.3 | 92.7 | 12.3 | 3 | 19 |
| 1946 | 1.3 | 55.2 | 15.1 | 2 | 9 |
| 1947 | 1.5 | 34.5 | 15.4 | 4 | 10 |
| 1948 | 1.2 | 29.8 | 17.7 | 4 | 7 |
| 1949 | 2.8 | 38.8 | 12.8 | 7 | 22 |
| 1950 | 3.0 | 42.6 | 13.6 | 7 | 22 |
| 1951 | 0.8 | 45.5 | 15.9 | 2 | 5 |
| 1952 | 1.2 | 67.7 | 15.0 | 2 | 8 |
| 1953 | 3.2 | 76.1 | 13.0 | 4 | 25 |
| 1954 | 2.6 | 70.9 | 12.4 | 4 | 21 |
| 1955 | 4.3 | 68.4 | 11.3 | 6 | 38 |
| 1956 | 4.8 | 70.6 | 11.3 | 7 | 42 |
| 1957 | 4.6 | 76.6 | 11.1 | 6 | 41 |
| 1958 | 4.4 | 82.4 | 13.2 | 5 | 33 |
| 1959 | 7.1 | 92.1 | 10.7 | 8 | 66 |
| 1960 | 5.4 | 92.2 | 11.5 | 6 | 47 |
| 1961 | 5.9 | 97.7 | 12.0 | 6 | 49 |
| 1962 | 6.7 | 106.8 | 12.1 | 6 | 55 |

## Table A-1 (continued)

| Year | USDA Outlays | Federal Outlays[1] | Net Farm Income | USDA Outlays as % of | |
|------|------|------|------|------|------|
| | | ($ Billions) | | Federal Outlays | Net Farm Income |
| 1963 | 7.7 | 111.3 | 11.8 | 7 | 65 |
| 1964 | 7.9 | 118.5 | 10.5 | 7 | 75 |
| 1965 | 6.8 | 118.2 | 12.9 | 6 | 53 |
| 1966 | 5.5 | 134.5 | 14.0 | 4 | 39 |
| 1967 | 5.8 | 157.5 | 12.3 | 4 | 47 |
| 1968 | 7.3 | 178.1 | 12.3 | 4 | 59 |
| 1969 | 8.3 | 183.6 | 14.3 | 5 | 58 |
| 1970 | 8.4 | 195.6 | 14.4 | 4 | 58 |
| 1971 | 8.6 | 210.2 | 15.0 | 4 | 57 |
| 1972 | 10.9 | 230.7 | 19.5 | 5 | 56 |
| 1973 | 11.4 | 245.7 | 34.4 | 5 | 33 |
| 1974 | 9.8 | 269.4 | 27.3 | 4 | 36 |
| 1975 | 15.6 | 332.3 | 25.5 | 5 | 62 |
| 1976 | 12.8 | 371.8 | 20.2 | 3 | 63 |
| 1977 | 16.7 | 409.2 | 19.9 | 4 | 84 |
| 1978 | 20.4 | 458.7 | 25.2 | 4 | 81 |
| 1979 | 31.8 | 503.5 | 27.4 | 6 | 118 |
| 1980 | 34.8 | 590.9 | 16.1 | 6 | 216 |
| 1981 | 41.6 | 678.2 | 26.9 | 8 | 155 |
| 1982 | 45.7 | 745.7 | 23.5 | 6 | 194 |
| 1983 | 52.4 | 808.3 | 12.7 | 6 | 413 |
| 1984 | 42.0 | 851.8 | 32.0 | 5 | 131 |
| 1985 | 55.5 | 946.3 | 32.3 | 6 | 172 |
| 1986 | 58.7 | 989.8 | 37.5 | 6 | 157 |

SOURCES: U.S. Department of Commerce, *Statistical Abstract of the United States; Economic Report of the President;* and U.S. Department of Agriculture, *Economic Indicators of the Farm Sector: National Financial Summary;* and *Farm Sector Review.*
[1]Includes off-budget outlays.

## Table A-2

### REALIZED GOVERNMENT LOSSES ON FARM PRICE, INCOME SUPPORT, AND RELATED PROGRAMS ($ MILLIONS)

| Year | Producer Payments | CCC Inventory Operations | Other[1] | Total Losses[2] Amount | % of Net Farm Income |
|------|------|------|------|------|------|
| 1933 | — | — | 75 | 75 | 3 |
| 1934 | — | 1 | 48 | 49 | 2 |
| 1935 | — | 1 | 178 | 179 | 3 |
| 1936 | — | 20 | 450 | 470 | 11 |
| 1937 | — | 9 | 434 | 443 | 7 |
| 1938 | — | 3 | 224 | 227 | 5 |
| 1939 | — | 8 | 582 | 590 | 13 |
| 1940 | — | 16 | 731 | 747 | 17 |
| 1941 | — | 36 | 730 | 766 | 12 |
| 1942 | — | − 79 | 714 | 635 | 6 |
| 1943 | — | − 36 | 548 | 512 | 4 |
| 1944 | — | − 8 | 410 | 402 | 3 |
| 1945 | — | 61 | − 11 | 50 | 0 |
| 1946 | — | − 33 | 57 | 24 | 0 |
| 1947 | — | − 157 | 106 | − 51 | 0 |
| 1948 | — | 81 | 36 | 117 | 1 |
| 1949 | — | 266 | 63 | 329 | 3 |
| 1950 | — | 294 | 193 | 487 | 4 |
| 1951 | — | 389 | 235 | 624 | 4 |
| 1952 | — | 103 | 203 | 306 | 2 |
| 1953 | — | 123 | 208 | 331 | 3 |
| 1954 | — | 546 | 108 | 654 | 5 |
| 1955 | — | 980 | 139 | 1,119 | 10 |
| 1956 | — | 1,139 | 275 | 1,414 | 13 |
| 1957 | — | 1,320 | 492 | 1,812 | 16 |
| 1958 | — | 1,086 | 562 | 1,648 | 12 |
| 1959 | — | 980 | 430 | 1,410 | 13 |
| 1960 | — | 971 | 914 | 1,885 | 16 |
| 1961 | 333 | 965 | 784 | 2,082 | 17 |
| 1962 | 868 | 1,235 | 696 | 2,799 | 23 |
| 1963 | 946 | 970 | 739 | 2,655 | 23 |
| 1964 | 1,285 | 1,147 | 795 | 3,227 | 31 |

## Table A-2 (continued)

| Year | Producer Payments | CCC Inventory Operations | Other[1] | Total Losses[2] | |
|------|------------------|--------------------------|----------|-----------------|--|
| | | | | Amount | % of Net Farm Income |
| 1965 | 1,608 | 871 | 569 | 3,048 | 24 |
| 1966 | 1,657 | 685 | 643 | 2,985 | 21 |
| 1967 | 2,458 | 764 | 591 | 3,813 | 31 |
| 1968 | 2,033 | 710 | 455 | 3,198 | 26 |
| 1969 | 2,146 | 411 | 556 | 3,113 | 22 |
| 1970 | 2,945 | 398 | 870 | 4,213 | 29 |
| 1971 | 2,909 | 316 | 833 | 4,058 | 27 |
| 1972 | 2,369 | 454 | 634 | 3,457 | 18 |
| 1973 | 3,122 | 161 | 811 | 4,094 | 12 |
| 1974 | 2,351 | 72 | 336 | 2,759 | 10 |
| 1975 | 560 | 114 | 36 | 710 | 3 |
| 1976 | 288 | 162 | 75 | 525 | 3 |
| 1977 | 594 | 108 | 122 | 824 | 4 |
| 1978 | 2,152 | 296 | 608 | 3,056 | 11 |
| 1979 | 1,928 | 333 | 1,039 | 3,300 | 10 |
| 1980 | 418 | 479 | 1,399 | 2,296 | 11 |
| 1981 | 1,030 | 926 | 1,575 | 3,531 | 12 |
| 1982 | 1,491 | 1,377 | 2,855 | 5,723 | 24 |
| 1983 | 4,734 | 2,562 | 12,217 | 19,513 | 154 |
| 1984 | 4,553 | 2,701 | 1,264 | 8,518 | 27 |
| 1985 | 7,308 | 3,620 | 2,007 | 12,935 | 40 |
| 1986 | 13,950 | 4,255 | 1,793 | 19,998 | 53 |

SOURCES: For 1933–53, Murray R. Benedict, *Can We Solve the Farm Problem?* (New York: Twentieth Century Fund, 1955), p. 557; for 1954 to date, U.S. Department of Agriculture, Agricultural Stabilization and Conservation Service, *Commodity Credit Corporation Charts: A Summary of Data through September 30, 1979;* and *Commodity Credit Corporation Report of Financial Condition and Operations.*

[1]Includes producer payments under the Agricultural Adjustment Act of 1933 and the soil bank program in addition to Payment-in-Kind program costs, grain reserve storage expenses, emergency feed program costs, loan and other charge-offs, interest expenses, and net operating expense.

[2]Excludes losses under P.L. 480, the National Wool Act, and export credit sales programs.

## Table A-3

### Direct Government Payments (Annual Average) by Program ($ Millions)

| Period | Conservation | Feed Grain | Wheat | Rice | Cotton | Wool | Miscellaneous[1] | Total |
|---|---|---|---|---|---|---|---|---|
| 1933–34 | 0 | 0 | 0 | 0 | 25 | 0 | 263 | 288 |
| 1935–39 | 237 | 0 | 0 | 0 | 36 | 0 | 207 | 479 |
| 1940–44 | 408 | 0 | 0 | 0 | 0 | 0 | 260 | 668 |
| 1945–49 | 239 | 0 | 0 | 0 | 0 | 0 | 215 | 454 |
| 1950–54 | 226 | 0 | 0 | 0 | 0 | 0 | 36 | 263 |
| 1955–59 | 217 | 0 | 0 | 0 | 0 | 41 | 456 | 714 |
| 1960–64 | 231 | 724 | 190 | 0 | 8 | 45 | 366 | 1,564 |
| 1965–69 | 225 | 1,312 | 708 | 0 | 678 | 42 | 251 | 3,215 |
| 1970–74 | 169 | 1,129 | 630 | 0 | 663 | 59 | 143 | 2,792 |
| 1975–79 | 233 | 466 | 435 | 38 | 129 | 23 | 228 | 1,553 |
| 1980–84 | 195 | 610 | 829 | 126 | 426 | 62 | 2,639 | 4,887 |
| 1985 | 189 | 2,861 | 1,950 | 577 | 1,106 | 98 | 924 | 7,704 |

Source: U.S. Department of Agriculture, *Economic Indicators of the Farm Sector: National Financial Summary*, 1985.
[1]Amounts are for soil bank program through 1970 and include the value of payment-in-kind commodities transferred to farmers under all other programs thereafter.

## Table A-4

### SUPPORT PRICE (SP)[1] AND MARKET PRICE FOR FARMERS (MP), MAJOR CROPS

| Year | Wheat ($ per bu.) SP | MP | Rice ($ per cwt.) SP | MP | Corn ($ per bu.) SP | MP | Cotton (¢ per lb.) SP | MP | Tobacco (¢ per lb.) SP[2] | MP | Soybeans ($ per bu.) SP | MP |
|---|---|---|---|---|---|---|---|---|---|---|---|---|
| 1933 | — | 0.74 | — | 1.73 | 0.45 | 0.52 | 10.0 | 10.2 | — | 13.0 | — | 0.94 |
| 1934 | — | 0.85 | — | 1.76 | 0.55 | 0.81 | 12.0 | 12.4 | — | 21.3 | — | 0.99 |
| 1935 | — | 0.83 | — | 1.60 | 0.45 | 0.66 | 10.0 | 11.1 | — | 18.4 | — | 0.73 |
| 1936 | — | 1.02 | — | 1.85 | 0.55 | 1.04 | — | 12.4 | — | 23.6 | — | 1.27 |
| 1937 | — | 0.96 | — | 1.46 | 0.50 | 0.52 | 9.0 | 8.4 | — | 20.4 | — | 0.85 |
| 1938 | 0.60 | 0.56 | — | 1.42 | 0.57 | 0.49 | 8.3 | 8.6 | — | 19.6 | — | 0.67 |
| 1939 | 0.63 | 0.69 | — | 1.62 | 0.57 | 0.57 | 8.7 | 9.1 | 15.4 | 15.4 | — | 0.81 |
| 1940 | 0.64 | 0.68 | — | 1.80 | 0.61 | 0.62 | 8.9 | 9.9 | 15.0 | 16.1 | — | 0.90 |
| 1941 | 0.98 | 0.94 | 2.06 | 3.01 | 0.75 | 0.75 | 14.0 | 17.0 | 19.6 | 26.4 | 1.05 | 1.55 |
| 1942 | 1.14 | 1.10 | 2.30 | 3.61 | 0.83 | 0.92 | 17.0 | 19.1 | 25.1 | 36.9 | 1.60 | 1.61 |
| 1943 | 1.23 | 1.36 | (³) | 3.96 | 0.90 | 1.12 | 18.4 | 19.9 | 27.6 | 40.5 | 1.80 | 1.81 |
| 1944 | 1.35 | 1.41 | (³) | 3.93 | 0.98 | 1.03 | 20.8 | 20.7 | 28.9 | 42.0 | 2.04 | 2.05 |
| 1945 | 1.38 | 1.49 | 2.82 | 3.98 | 1.01 | 1.23 | 20.9 | 22.5 | 29.7 | 42.6 | 2.04 | 2.08 |
| 1946 | 1.49 | 1.90 | (⁴) | 5.00 | 1.15 | 1.53 | 22.8 | 32.6 | 32.1 | 45.1 | 2.04 | 2.57 |
| 1947 | 1.84 | 2.29 | 3.76 | 5.97 | 1.37 | 2.16 | 26.5 | 31.9 | 40.0 | 43.6 | 2.04 | 3.33 |
| 1948 | 2.00 | 1.98 | 4.09 | 4.88 | 1.44 | 1.28 | 28.8 | 30.4 | 43.9 | 48.2 | 2.18 | 2.27 |
| 1949 | 1.95 | 1.88 | 3.96 | 4.10 | 1.40 | 1.24 | 27.2 | 28.6 | 42.5 | 47.2 | 2.11 | 2.16 |
| 1950 | 1.99 | 2.00 | 4.56 | 5.09 | 1.47 | 1.52 | 27.9 | 40.1 | 45.0 | 54.7 | 2.06 | 2.47 |

## Table A-4 (continued)

| Year | Wheat ($ per bu.) SP | MP | Rice ($ per cwt.) SP | MP | Corn ($ per bu.) SP | MP | Cotton (¢ per lb.) SP | MP | Tobacco (¢ per lb.) SP² | MP | Soybeans ($ per bu.) SP | MP |
|------|------|------|------|------|------|------|------|------|------|------|------|------|
| 1951 | 2.18 | 2.11 | 5.00 | 4.82 | 1.57 | 1.66 | 30.5 | 37.9 | 50.7 | 52.4 | 2.45 | 2.73 |
| 1952 | 2.20 | 2.09 | 5.04 | 5.87 | 1.60 | 1.52 | 30.9 | 34.6 | 50.6 | 50.3 | 2.56 | 2.72 |
| 1953 | 2.21 | 2.04 | 4.84 | 5.19 | 1.60 | 1.48 | 30.8 | 32.3 | 47.9 | 52.8 | 2.56 | 2.72 |
| 1954 | 2.24 | 2.12 | 4.92 | 4.57 | 1.62 | 1.43 | 31.6 | 33.6 | 47.9 | 52.7 | 2.22 | 2.46 |
| 1955 | 2.08 | 1.98 | 4.66 | 4.81 | 1.58 | 1.35 | 31.7 | 32.3 | 48.3 | 52.7 | 2.04 | 2.22 |
| 1956 | 2.00 | 1.97 | 4.57 | 4.86 | 1.50 | 1.29 | 29.3 | 31.7 | 48.9 | 51.5 | 2.15 | 2.18 |
| 1957 | 2.00 | 1.93 | 4.72 | 5.11 | 1.40 | 1.11 | 28.8 | 29.6 | 50.8 | 55.4 | 2.09 | 2.07 |
| 1958 | 1.82 | 1.75 | 4.48 | 4.68 | 1.36 | 1.12 | 31.2 | 33.2 | 54.6 | 58.2 | 2.09 | 2.00 |
| 1959 | 1.81 | 1.76 | 4.38 | 4.59 | 1.12 | 1.05 | 30.4 | 31.7 | 55.5 | 58.3 | 1.85 | 1.96 |
| 1960 | 1.78 | 1.74 | 4.42 | 4.55 | 1.06 | 1.00 | 29.0 | 30.2 | 55.5 | 60.4 | 1.85 | 2.13 |
| 1961 | 1.79 | 1.83 | 4.71 | 5.10 | 1.20 | 1.10 | 33.0 | 32.9 | 55.5 | 64.3 | 2.30 | 2.28 |
| 1962 | 2.00 | 2.04 | 4.71 | 5.04 | 1.20 | 1.12 | 32.5 | 31.9 | 56.1 | 60.1 | 2.25 | 2.34 |
| 1963 | 2.00 | 1.85 | 4.71 | 5.01 | 1.25 | 1.11 | 32.5 | 32.2 | 56.6 | 58.0 | 2.25 | 2.51 |
| 1964 | 2.00 | 1.37 | 4.71 | 4.90 | 1.25 | 1.17 | 33.5 | 29.8 | 57.2 | 58.5 | 2.25 | 2.62 |
| 1965 | 2.00 | 1.35 | 4.50 | 4.93 | 1.25 | 1.16 | 33.3 | 28.1 | 57.7 | 64.6 | 2.25 | 2.54 |
| 1966 | 2.57 | 1.63 | 4.50 | 4.95 | 1.30 | 1.24 | 30.4 | 20.8 | 58.8 | 66.9 | 2.50 | 2.75 |
| 1967 | 2.61 | 1.39 | 4.55 | 4.97 | 1.35 | 1.03 | 31.8 | 25.6 | 59.9 | 64.2 | 2.50 | 2.49 |
| 1968 | 2.63 | 1.24 | 4.60 | 5.00 | 1.35 | 1.08 | 32.5 | 22.1 | 61.6 | 66.6 | 2.50 | 2.43 |
| 1969 | 2.77 | 1.25 | 4.72 | 4.95 | 1.35 | 1.16 | 35.0 | 22.0 | 63.8 | 71.8 | 2.25 | 2.35 |
| 1970 | 2.82 | 1.33 | 4.86 | 5.17 | 1.35 | 1.33 | 37.1 | 22.0 | 66.6 | 72.9 | 2.25 | 2.85 |

## Table A-4 (continued)

| Year | Wheat ($ per bu.) | | Rice ($ per cwt.) | | Corn ($ per bu.) | | Cotton (¢ per lb.) | | Tobacco (¢ per lb.) | | Soybeans ($ per bu.) | |
|---|---|---|---|---|---|---|---|---|---|---|---|---|
| | SP | MP | SP | MP | SP | MP | SP | MP | SP² | MP | SP | MP |
| 1971 | 2.93 | 1.34 | 5.07 | 5.34 | 1.35 | 1.08 | 35.0 | 28.2 | 69.4 | 78.6 | 2.25 | 3.03 |
| 1972 | 3.02 | 1.76 | 5.27 | 6.73 | 1.41 | 1.57 | 35.8 | 27.3 | 72.7 | 83.0 | 2.25 | 4.37 |
| 1973 | 3.39 | 3.95 | 6.07 | 13.80 | 1.64 | 2.55 | 41.5 | 44.6 | 76.6 | 90.1 | 2.25 | 5.68 |
| 1974 | 2.05 | 4.09 | 7.54 | 11.20 | 1.38 | 3.02 | 38.0 | 42.9 | 83.3 | 108.6 | 2.25 | 6.64 |
| 1975 | 2.05 | 3.55 | 8.52 | 8.35 | 1.38 | 2.54 | 38.0 | 51.3 | 93.2 | 102.6 | — | 4.92 |
| 1976 | 2.29 | 2.73 | 8.25 | 7.02 | 1.57 | 2.15 | 43.2 | 64.1 | 106.0 | 112.5 | 2.50 | 6.81 |
| 1977 | 2.90 | 2.33 | 8.25 | 9.49 | 2.00 | 2.02 | 47.8 | 52.3 | 113.8 | 118.6 | 3.50 | 5.88 |
| 1978 | 3.40 | 2.97 | 8.57 | 8.16 | 2.10 | 2.25 | 52.0 | 58.4 | 121.0 | 132.4 | 4.50 | 6.66 |
| 1979 | 3.40 | 3.78 | 9.05 | 10.50 | 2.20 | 2.52 | 57.7 | 62.5 | 129.3 | 141.1 | 4.50 | 6.28 |
| 1980 | 3.63 | 3.91 | 9.49 | 12.80 | 2.35 | 3.10 | 58.4 | 74.7 | 141.5 | 152.3 | 5.02 | 7.57 |
| 1981 | 3.81 | 3.66 | 10.68 | 9.05 | 2.40 | 2.50 | 70.9 | 54.3 | 158.7 | 170.6 | 5.02 | 6.04 |
| 1982 | 4.05 | 3.55 | 10.85 | 8.11 | 2.70 | 2.68 | 71.0 | 59.1 | 169.9 | 176.4 | 5.02 | 5.69 |
| 1983 | 4.30 | 3.53 | 11.40 | 8.76 | 2.86 | 3.25 | 76.0 | 66.0 | 169.9 | 174.6 | 5.02 | 7.81 |
| 1984 | 4.38 | 3.38 | 11.90 | 8.06 | 3.03 | 2.62 | 81.0 | 57.5 | 169.9 | 180.6 | 5.02 | 5.78 |
| 1985 | 4.38 | 3.08 | 11.90 | 6.53 | 3.03 | 2.23 | 81.0 | 56.5 | 169.9 | 171.9 | 5.02 | 5.05 |
| 1986 | 4.38 | 2.42 | 11.90 | 3.80 | 3.03 | 1.45 | 81.0 | 51.5 | 143.8 | 152.7 | 4.77 | 4.67 |
| 1987 | 4.38 | — | 11.66 | — | 3.03 | — | 79.4 | — | 143.5 | — | — | — |

SOURCE: U.S. Department of Agriculture, *Agricultural Statistics*, 1956, 1962, 1972, 1984, and 1987.

[1] National average of loan rate plus direct support payments.

[2] SP for flu-cured types 11–14. Prior to 1949 average price received by farmers for all types.

[3] Loan rate not announced.

[4] Loan rate not announced, although supports mandatory.

# Index

AAA. *See* Agricultural Adjustment
   Administration
Acreage reduction program (*see also*
   Direct payments; Price supports)
   circumvention techniques, 31–32, 41
   controls, tightening of, 44–45
   cotton market, effect on, 34–36
   countervailing policies, 38, 39–40
   efforts by AAA, 16, 18–19
   noncontrolled crops, increase under,
      23, 25, 32
   and soil fertility, 31
Agricultural Act of 1949, 93
Agricultural Act of 1954, 44
Agricultural Act of 1956, 44
Agricultural Act of 1965, 56
Agricultural Act of 1970, 56
Agricultural Act of 1985, 59
Agricultural Adjustment Act, 13–15,
   27–28, 33
Agricultural Adjustment
   Administration (AAA)
   Consumers Council, 62
   creation of, 13–14
   dairy products under, 91
   farm productivity under, 22 tbl, 24 tbl
   production reduction efforts, 16, 18–
      19
Agricultural and Consumer Protection
   Act of 1973, 56
Agricultural Credit Act of 1921, 70
Agricultural Credit Act of 1978, 74–75
Agricultural Marketing Act of 1929, 6
Agricultural Marketing Agreement Act
   of 1937, 91–93
Agricultural Trade Development and
   Assistance Act of 1954. *See* Public
   Law 480
Agriculture
   crop surpluses, *see* Surplus stocks
   farmers' response to acreage
      reduction program, 23, 25, 31–32,
      41
   and market forces argument, 2–3, 10,
      44

production reduction efforts by
   AAA, 16, 18–19, 22 tbl, 24 tbl
productivity increases, 55
research and education expansion, 38
soil enrichment trends, 38, 39 tbl
Agriculture, Department of. *See* U.S.
   Department of Agriculture
Agriculture Extension Services, 38
American Cotton Cooperative
   Association, 7
American Institute of Banking, 85
Anderson, Clinton P., 45

Bankhead-Jones Farm Tenancy Act of
   1937, 19
Banks for Cooperatives, 69
Benson, Ezra Taft, 27, 43–44, 45, 48
Black, John D., 2
Brannan Plan, 45n

Capper-Volstead Act of 1922, 91, 96
Cattlemen's Association, 89
CCC. *See* Commodity Credit
   Corporation
Christopherson Bill, 3
Citizens Board of Inquiry, 63
Coca-Cola, 106, 108
Commodity Credit Corporation (CCC),
   15
   commodity loan rates, 46 tbl
   holdings of major commodities,
      26 tbl
Commodity markets (*see also* Direct
   payments; Price supports)
   AAA production reduction efforts,
      16, 18–19, 22 tbl, 24 tbl
   CCC loan rates, 46 tbl
   early intervention proposals, 3–6
   government-assisted exports, 49
   import quotas and, 33n
   merchandising and consumption
      subsidies, 47

parity concept introduced, 13–15
price stabilization efforts during
  Depression, 7–9
subsidized farm credit, effect on, 86
support prices, 35 tbl, 37
surpluses and CCC, 25, 27–28
two-price plan, 4–6, 10
Common Market, 97n
Conservation Reserve program, 44
Coolidge, Calvin, 5
Corn
  acreage, yield, and production
    changes, 22 tbl, 23, 24 tbl
  CCC holdings, 26 tbl
  CCC loan rates, 46 tbl
  support price and market price, 141–
    43 tbl
  support prices, 35 tbl, 37
Corn sweeteners (see also Sugar)
  consumption increases, 102, 106–108
  high-fructose, prices of, 108 tbl
  as sugar competitor, 106–108, 109–
    110, 111
  U.S. consumption of, 103 tbl
  U.S. production, imports, and
    consumption, 107 tbl
Cotton
  acreage, yield, and production
    changes, 22 tbl, 24 tbl, 25
  CCC holdings, 26 tbl
  CCC loan rates, 46 tbl
  direct government payments, 140 tbl
  market-certificate export subsidy, 59
  price stabilization program, 8–9
  price supports, 34–37, 141–43 tbl
  processing taxes on, 15–16n
  skip-row-planting technique, 31
  synthetic fibers, competition from,
    35n, 36
  U.S. and world exports, 36 tbl
  upland, production and exports, 34
    tbl
Cotton Stabilization Corporation, 8
Credit. See Farm Credit

Dairy products, 89–97
  DTP, 89, 91
  government purchases of, 90 tbl
  milk marketing orders, 92–93, 96
  perishability factor and price, 94–95
  price support efforts, 16–17, 91–93
  school lunch milk program, 47
  surpluses of, 27, 93–94

trade barriers, 93, 97n
Dairy Termination Program (DTP), 89,
  91
Depression. See Great Depression
Developing countries
  food donations, effect of, 50
  free trade, effects on, 128
  sugar policies, effect on, 109
Direct payments (see also Acreage
  reduction program; Price supports)
  to all farmers, 125, 127
  costs and benefits revealed, 57–58
  distribution disparities, 117–19, 120
  by program, 140 tbl
  by sales class, 118 tbl
DTP (Dairy Termination Program), 89,
  91

Economic Opportunity Act of 1964, 74
Eisenhower, Dwight D., 43–44, 46
Emergency Livestock Credit Act of
  1974, 74
Equality for Agriculture, 4
Exports (see also Imports)
  agricultural, commercial and
    government-assisted, 49 tbl
  agricultural, increase of, 58
  bounty bill (1895), 1
  cotton, effect of price supports on,
    34–36
  Public Law 480, effects of, 48–51
  subsidy for cotton and rice, 59

Farm credit
  CCC loan rates, 46 tbl
  delinquencies, 83–84
  efficiency, effect on, 84–85
  excesses, results of, 79–81
  farm non–real estate debt, 73 tbl
  farm real estate debt, 72 tbl, 78
  FLB rates, 78–79
  FmHA emergency loans, 71n, 74–75
  history of, 69–71, 74–75
  land value increase from, 77–79
  New Deal actions, 19, 40–41, 71
  productivity, effect on, 81–82
  subsidized credit expansion, 77
Farm Credit Act of 1971, 78
Farm Credit Administration, 9n, 69
Farm Credit System (FCS)
  creation of, 69–70
  expansion of, 77–79

losses and bailout, 80–81, 87
Farm income
  and direct payments, 57–58
  diversity of, 113
  by farm, 114 tbl
  federal outlays for, 119 tbl
  and labor supply, 115–16
  USDA outlays and, 136–37 tbl
Farm Loan Act of 1916, 40
Farm Security Administration, 19, 41,
  71 (see also Farmers Home
  Administration)
Farmers Home Administration (FmHA)
  active loans, 76 tbl, 78
  delinquency rates, 83–84
  effects on private lenders, 85–86
  emergency loans, 71n, 74–75
  farm non–real estate debt, 73 tbl
  farm real estate debt, 72 tbl, 81
  history of, 19, 41, 71, 74
  rural aid loans, 71, 74
Farmers National Council, 3
Farmers National Grain Corporation, 7,
  8
Farmland
  price supports, effect on value, 116–
  17
  value increase from credit, 77–79
FCS. See Farm Credit System
Federal Deposit Insurance Corporation
  (FDIC), 80, 81n
Federal Farm Board, 6–9, 10–11, 62
Federal Farm Loan Act of 1916, 69
Federal Intermediate Credit Banks, 40,
  69
Federal Land Bank Associations, 69
Federal Land Banks (FLBs), 40, 69, 78–
  79
Federal Savings and Loan Association
  Insurance Corporation (FSLIC), 81n
Federal Surplus Commodities
  Corporation, 61
Federal Surplus Relief Corporation, 61,
  62
FLBs (Federal Land Banks), 40, 69, 78–
  79
Flexible price supports, 45–47
FmHA. See Farmers Home
  Administration
Food and Agricultural Act of 1977, 56n
Food for Peace Act. See Public Law 480
Food Security Act of 1985, 94
Food Stamp Act of 1964, 61, 62
Food stamp program, 47, 61–68

The Food Stamp Program: History,
  Description, Issues and Options, 63
Foreign economic development. See
  Developing countries
FSLIC (Federal Savings and Loan
  Association Insurance Corporation),
  81n

Galbraith, John Kenneth, 46
Gardner, Bruce, 121–22, 123
General Agreement on Trade and
  Tariffs (GATT), 97n
Gooding Bill, 4
Grain sorghum
  CCC holdings, 26 tbl
  CCC loan rates, 46 tbl
  and PIK scheme, 58–59
  support prices, 35 tbl, 37
Great Depression (see also New Deal
  programs)
  agricultural distress, 13
  price stabilization efforts during, 7–9

Housing Act of 1970, 74
Hunger USA, 63

Imports (see also Exports)
  commodity quotas, 33n
  dairy products quotas, 93, 97n
  sugar, 100 tbl
  sugar quotas, 99n, 102, 104–106, 109,
  110
  sugar tariffs, 16, 99, 102, 109
  wool tariffs, 17
International Harvester Company, 2n,
  6
International Wheat Agreement, 52

Johnson, Hugh S., 4
Jones-Costigan Act of 1934, 16, 102

Ladd-Sinclair Bill, 4
Legge, Alexander, 2, 2n
Liechtenstein, Prince of, 113
Little Bill, 4
Long, Russell, 104n
Lubin, David, 1

Marijuana cultivation, 109
Market forces (*see also* Commodity markets)
  agricultural exemption argument, 2–3, 10, 44
  and aid to farmers, 45–46
McNary-Haugen Bills, 5–6
Meat products, production reduction efforts, 16
Milk. *See* Dairy products
Moline Plow Company, 4

National Bean Marketing Association, 7
National Beet Growers Association, 7
National Fruit and Vegetable Exchange, 7
National Grange, 1
National Livestock Marketing Association, 7
National Pecan Marketing Association, 7
National Recovery Administrations, 62
National Wool Act, 52
National Wool Marketing Corporation, 7
New Deal programs
  farm productivity under, 21–25, 31–32
  parity, birth of, 13–17
  production reduction efforts, 17–19
Nixon, Richard M., 66
Norris Bill, 3
Norris-Sinclair Bill, 3
Nourse, Edwin G., 3, 3n

Oats, acreage, yield, and production changes, 22 tbl, 24 tbl
Omnibus Farm Bill of 1985, 109

Parity concept
  birth of, 13–15
  formula, 33
  Public Law 480 dilemma, 48
Payment-in-Kind (PIK) system, 58–59, 117
Peanuts
  CCC loan rates, 46 tbl
  support prices, 35 tbl, 37
Peek, George N., 4

PIK (Payment-in-Kind) system, 58–59, 117
Poor People's Campaign, 66
Poverty
  in developing countries, 50
  of farmers, 125–27
  measures of, 117–19
  subsidized farm credit, effect on, 86
  and surplus food distribution, 62–63, 66–67
  of U. S. and farm families, 126 tbl
Price supports (*see also* Acreage reduction program; Direct payments; Commodity markets)
  and commodity surpluses, 25, 27–28
  cotton market, effect on, 34–36
  dairy products, 91–94
  during Depression, 7–9, 10–11
  flexible, 45–47
  government losses from, 28–29, 51–52, 120–21, 138–39 tbl
  and import quotas, 32, 33n
  land values, effect on, 116–17
  McNary-Haugen Bills, 5–6
  milk diversion payments, 95 tbl
  New Deal programs, 13–17
  origin of, 1–4
  "parity ratio" formula, 33
  Peek-Johnson proposal, 4–6
  Public Law 480 parity dilemma, 48
  social costs of, 121–24
  sugar, 102, 104–106, 109–110, 111
  target pricing, 56–58, 117
  in World War II, 37
Production Credit Associations, 69
Productivity increases on farms, 55, 81–82
Public Law 480
  "dumping" effect, 50–51
  effect on developing countries, 50
  government losses from, 51–52
  parity dilemma from, 48
  purpose of, 47

Quotas, import (*see also* Tariffs)
  commodity, 33n
  dairy products, 93, 97n
  sugar, 99n, 102, 104–106, 109, 110

Reciprocal Trade Agreements Act of 1934, 32
Red Cross, 61, 62
Resettlement Administration, 40, 71

Reuther, Walter, 66n
Rice
    acreage, yield, and production
        changes, 22 tbl, 24 tbl, 25
    direct government payments, 140 tbl
    market-certificate export subsidy, 59
    support price and market price, 141–
        43 tbl
    support prices, 35 tbl, 37
Roosevelt, Franklin D., 13
Rural Development Act of 1972, 74

School lunch milk program, 47
School lunch program, 63
Senior Citizens Housing Act of 1962, 71
Smoot-Hawley Tariff Act of 1930, 32
Smoot, Reed, 62
Soil Bank program, 44–45, 55
Soil Conservation and Domestic
    Allotment Act of 1936, 16, 16n, 18–19
Soil Conservation Service, 19, 38, 74
Soybeans
    acreage, yield, and production
        changes, 22 tbl, 24 tbl, 25
    CCC holdings, 26 tbl
    support price and market price, 141–
        43 tbl
    support prices, 35 tbl, 37
Stigler, George, 127
Sugar (see also Corn sweeteners)
    acreage, yield, and production by
        state, 101 tbl
    acreage, yield, and production
        changes, 24 tbl
    average price of, 105 tbl
    import quotas for, 99n, 102, 104–106,
        109, 110
    import tariffs for, 16, 99, 102, 109
    refined, prices of, 108 tbl
    subsidization, impact on prices, 104–
        106
    U.S. consumption of, 103 tbl
    U.S. production, 99–102
    U.S. production, imports, and
        consumption, 107 tbl
Supply management. See Acreage
    reduction program
Supreme Court, 15n
Surplus stocks
    CCC holdings, 25–28
    and food subsidy programs, 47, 62–
        63
    PIK scheme for, 58–59

Public Law 480, effect of, 47–50
Sweeteners. See Corn sweeteners;
    Sugar

Target pricing system, 56–58, 117
Tariffs (see also Quotas)
    sugar, 16, 99, 102, 109
    wool, 17
Taylor, Henry C., 6
Tenant labor, 116
Thompson, John G., 2
Tobacco
    acreage, yield, and production
        changes, 22 tbl, 24 tbl, 25
    CCC holdings, 26 tbl
    support price and market price, 141–
        43 tbl
    support prices, 35 tbl, 37
Trade barriers, removal of, 32–33, 128

U.S. Department of Agriculture
    (USDA)
    DTP program, 89, 91
    farm subsidy costs, 29, 51–52, 136–37
        tbl
    milk marketing orders, 92–93, 96
U.S. Supreme Court, 15n

Veblen, Thorstein, 13

Wallace, Henry A., 13, 13n, 17–18, 45
Wallace, Henry C., 4–5
War Finance Corporation, 70
Water Facilities Act of 1954, 71
Wheat
    acreage, yield, and production
        changes, 22 tbl, 24 tbl, 25
    CCC holdings, 26 tbl
    CCC loan rates, 46 tbl
    direct government payments, 140 tbl
    early price support measures, 4, 8
    support price and market price, 141–
        43 tbl
    support prices, 35 tbl, 37
Wheat Growers Association, 5
Wilson, Woodrow, 69
Wool
    direct government payments, 140 tbl
    import tariffs on, 17

149

# About the Author

Clifton B. Luttrell was a specialist in agricultural economics at the Federal Reserve Bank of St. Louis from 1947 to 1982. Besides serving as a senior writer and editor of the bank's *Review*, he has published numerous articles on agricultural and monetary affairs in other leading economic journals. Luttrell studied at the University of Tennessee, the University of Illinois, and the University of Chicago.

# Cato Institute

Founded in 1977, the Cato Institute is a public policy research foundation dedicated to broadening the parameters of policy debate to allow consideration of more options that are consistent with the traditional American principles of limited government, individual liberty, and peace. Toward that goal, the Institute strives to achieve a greater involvement of the intelligent, concerned lay public in questions of policy and the proper role of government.

The Institute is named for *Cato's Letters*, pamphlets that were widely read in the American Colonies in the early 18th century and played a major role in laying the philosophical foundation for the revolution that followed. Since that revolution, civil and economic liberties have been eroded as the number and complexity of social problems have grown.

To counter this trend the Cato Institute undertakes an extensive publications program dealing with the complete spectrum of policy issues. Books, monographs, and shorter studies are commissioned to examine the federal budget, Social Security, regulation, NATO, international trade, and a myriad of other issues. Major policy conferences are held throughout the year, from which papers are published thrice yearly in the *Cato Journal*.

In order to maintain an independent posture, the Cato Institute accepts no government funding. Contributions are received from foundations, corporations, and individuals, and other revenue is generated from the sale of publications. The Institute is a nonprofit, tax-exempt, educational foundation under Section 501(c)3 of the Internal Revenue Code.

CATO INSTITUTE
224 Second St., S.E.
Washington, D.C. 20003